BY JULIAN VOIGT

THE SECRET TO THAT

TAKEAWAY CURRY TASTE

LEARN HOW TO COOK RESTAURANT & TAKEAWAY STYLE INDIAN CURRY

PART 2

THE SECRET TO THAT TAKEAWAY CURRY TASTE
PART 2

Disclaimer
All claims in this publication cannot be verified or proven.
All terms used in this publication should not be taken as literal,
e.g. 'authentic', 'Indian', 'BIR'.

Printed by CreateSpace, An Amazon.com Company

ISBN-13:9781519490674
ISBN-10:1519490674

Because of the dynamic nature of the Internet, any web addresses or
links contained in this book may have changed since publication and
may no longer be valid. The views expressed in this work are solely those
of the author and do not necessarily reflect the views of the publisher,
and the publisher hereby disclaims any responsibility for them.

CONTENTS

Chapter 7 - More Insights, Tips and Recipes 122

All good things come to an end 131
Final thoughts...135

ACKNOWLEDGEMENTS

I just want to say a **huge** thank you to the following people:

Firstly, thanks to Adey for his enthusiasm and commitment to this project - I know he is one seriously busy man, yet he always gave 100% in helping me to deliver the final product. My gratitude for his friendship and incredible work ethic that has driven his passion to perfect his art.

Next, I want to thank Anthony Paterson who evolved from Curry lover and reader of my first e-book to critic, adviser and eventually editor and PDF designer. To be honest, I couldn't have completed this project without his help. His ability to spot errors and his mental acuity, not only helped me create a better revision of my first e-book but also this *greater* work; Part 2. I am also grateful for his commitment, honesty and integrity!

Also, I would like to thank Mick Gay for his advice, cover design and cameraman duties over the past 16-months. Much appreciation for sticking out the 12 hour days and committing to the project.

A *special* thank you to Katy for putting up with yet another scheme - I bet she thought those crazy curry days were over, yet they crept back in! I am indebted for her never failing support and belief in all my dreams and schemes.

Lastly, I want to thank all those kind and thoughtful people who took the time to send their best wishes to Katy and myself when we were going through that particularly difficult time - believe me, your thoughts and expressions were very much appreciated. Also thanks to all those who send their expressions of appreciation for the videos, e-books etc. - even though I can't possibly reply to every e-mail please know that I read and appreciated them all!

Julian Voigt

KEY, CONVENTIONS and MEASURES & CONVERSIONS

Key

 This symbol is used to indicate there is a supporting YouTube video which can be viewed by clicking the icon with the LH Mouse Key.

> This symbol is used to identify 'Top Tip' Boxes that are filled with tips and techniques that many other recipe books leave out – tips and techniques that I wanted to include to give you that edge.

Conventions

I have tried to consistently 'standardise' the way information is presented and you will note that the recipes show the ingredient, followed by the quantity in round brackets in blue text, additional information, if required, is shown in curly brackets and OPTIONAL ingredients are identified by 'OPTIONAL', in red, within square brackets; eg:

Kalonji Seeds (½ tsp) {Onion Seeds} [OPTIONAL]

Use of Coloured Borders

Top Tips

Ingredients

Method

Ingredients & Method

I also employ colour text to easily identify certain ingredients like **Red Peppers**, Green Peppers and Green Chillis.

TBSP v tsp - To avoid confusion Tablespoons (TBSP) are shown in UPPERCASE and teaspoons (tsp) are shown in lower case. To indicate a 'HEAPED' measure then the measure is pre-fixed by an "H/ or h/" – eg H/TBSP and h/tsp.

Measures & Conversions
Ladle = 150ml
Chef Spoon = 30ml = 2 TBSP = 6 tsp
1 TBSP = 15ml = ½ Chef's Spoon = 3 tsp
1 tsp = 5ml
½ tsp = 2.5ml

Small Measures
½ tsp = 2 Tads
Tad = ¼ tsp = 2 Dashes
Dash = ½ Tad = 2 Pinches
Pinch = ½ Dash = 2 Smidgens
Smidgen = ½ Pinch = 2 Drops
Drop = ½ Smidgen = 2 Hints

Small measures are ideal for fine control of Chilli Powder, Salt and food colouring.

The set above can be bought from the USA on ebay for £3.322014. A word of caution - other sellers are selling the same for about double the price!

Search ebay for "Norpro measuring spoons"

Chapter 1

The 'Mancunian Way'

With my first exploration into the colourful world of British Indian Restaurant {BIR} curry being of the Manchester 'Curry Mile' version, that version came to be, for me a sort of benchmark by which I would measure all other 'Curry Houses', particularly in other parts of the UK. I was always curious to learn on my travels if these other 'Curry Houses' were as good as the ones back in Manchester.

When I began courting my wife back in the early 90's I was doing a lot of travelling to Blackpool where she lived. In the early days I couldn't wait to try what Blackpool had to offer with regards to 'Curry Houses' - I was disappointed!

Back then, the 'Indian' restaurants in and around Blackpool served up curries that, in my opinion, were watery and lacked flavour. I had become so accustomed to the Manchester version. Now I realise that there were no doubt a few reasons for the variance; Firstly, the restaurants in Rusholme Manchester I had grown up with were predominantly Pakistani owned and run, where as the ones I visited in Blackpool and a few other places were Bangladeshi. Also, the restaurants on Manchester's 'Curry Mile' served a large Asian community, whereas the ones I came across in Blackpool served mostly the English community and tourists, hence the difference.

Don't get me wrong, I am not saying that the Pakistani version of BIR is better than the Bangladeshi. Some of my favourite 'Indian' restaurants are Bengali run and it is true that amongst the Asian community the Bengalis are considered to be the "best cooks".

However, my preferred BIR style curry is and will always be Pakistani. Why? Because it's what I grew up with and the Pakistani style of BIR has a taste all of its own, which we will explore to some degree in this book.

As I travelled around the country it soon became obvious that most 'Indian' restaurants and takeaways are in fact run by the Bengali community and they are the ones who I guess deserve the most credit for, not just the invention of BIR style curry in the first place but also its constant evolution into curry most of us Brits know and love. The only two other places in the UK where I have noticed the Pakistani domination of the BIR scene over the Bengali are in Bradford and Glasgow.

The Manchester 'Curry Mile' therefore is quite unique in that it is predominantly Pakistani run and owned, in fact most of the Manchester curry scene is, Pakistani. Places like, Longsight, Levenshulme, Fallowfield, Oldham and Cheetham Hill, are all dominated by the Pakistani BIR scene.

In the so called 'Birmingham Balti Triangle' you will find mainly Bangladeshi run restaurants and takeaways with certain pockets that are exclusively Pakistani. For some reason, the two communities do not mix.

Having said all of that, and hopefully not having stereotyped any particular community, I have noticed that even on Wilmslow Rd in Manchester there are some Indian owned BIR restaurants like the *Shere Khan* and the *Royal Naz*, which also serve up their own particular great variety of BIR. These establishments are generally run by the Seekh community. One of the best Madras curries I have ever tasted, which wasn't that long ago actually, came from an Indian owned and run restaurant called the *'Punjab Tandoori Restaurant'*. This restaurant is nothing to look at from the outside {or the inside for that matter} but the food there is out of this world!

I wanted to try it with it being one of the few *real* Indian restaurants on the 'Curry Mile'. I thought that being nestled, as it was in between all the Pakistani competition it must have something to offer. I wasn't wrong!

I took my son Jacob there as a pre-match treat as we were looking to kill some time before the Man City v Birmingham City game. I ordered a vegetarian speciality - Malai Kofta and Jacob ordered the Chicken Madras; both were delicious, but the gravy that came with the Madras I can only describe as sublime! It was rich and saucy with the correct level of spice, yet the sauce wasn't dense and overpowering as it sometimes can be with this curry; rather it was light and fresh tasting. I wondered as I savoured this delightful version of one of my favourite curries - 'How have they achieved that taste'?

I was so impressed with this curry that a few weeks later I took my wife there one afternoon and we both had the Madras and I can tell you it was every bit as good as at the first visit! Again, as I ate the curry, I puzzled over how they had achieved this particular taste. What we both agreed on, after some deliberations - {*the waiters must have thought we were from the Environmental Health the way we were dissecting those curries*} - was that the Base Gravy had been made with fresh tomatoes and it was obvious too, that tomato purée hadn't come near these curries. Katy and I also detected the use of whole spices - "perhaps a wee sprinkling of Panch Puran"?

I plan on seeing if I can get the owner to reveal some of their 'secrets' to me because my two visits to this somewhat dowdy looking little restaurant presented to me a version of Chicken Madras, up until this point I had never experienced, or anything remotely like it, it was quite simply - the best Madras ever!

The 'Curry Mile'

According to Wikipedia - the Manchester 'Curry Mile' has the largest concentration of 'Indian' restaurants outside the Indian subcontinent with as many as 70 individual restaurants along the strip, which in actuality is less than a mile in length.

The Punjab Tandoori Restaurant

Here is a little bit of History about Manchester's famous 'Curry Mile', which I feel compelled to write about as it has had such an influence on my own 'Curry Journey'.

Was this the first Indian Restaurant on the 'Curry Mile'?

Back in 1959 the New Taj Mahal was, according to Manchester's Town Hall archives, the first Indian restaurant to open its doors for service to the residents of Rusholme. This little restaurant was nestled between a very 'English' tea shop and a laundrette. Today the Shere Khan stands in its place.

The New Taj Mahal

The Shere Khan

Even though it was the Indian community that first got a foothold on Manchester's Wilmslow road, it later came to be the Pakistani community that expanded the strip with many cafes and restaurant as well as kebab houses. A Famous 'Curry Mile' restaurant that has been there over forty years and is still popular is the Sanam.

Sanam

The Sanam is a large restaurant with two floors, an open plan kitchen annex and an adjacent 'Sweet Shop.' This restaurant back in the 1980's according to my opinion, served the best Vindaloo around!

The Lamb Vindaloo served up in the 1980's at the Sanam was quite simply the *best* Curry I can ever remember eating. Whether that was because I hadn't, at that stage experienced many alternatives, or whether it was because the resident Chef at that time was a 'genius' I don't know. All I can remember about that Curry was how *satisfying and tasty* it was. Yes it was hot and spicy but there was a lot more going on in it! The individual spices delicately coated your palate as opposed to assaulting them and the gravy that came with this Lamb Vindaloo had a meaty taste that was almost reminiscent of a well-cooked stew.

As the years rolled on I gradually noticed that the curries the Sanam served changed and the taste I had loved about the Sanam curries, seemed no longer to be there. It's some years since my last visit to the Sanam and I am now looking forward to re-visiting it again in the hope of maybe recapturing that taste.

One reason for the high standard of the curries in Manchester is the fact that originally those restaurants were opened to serve the Asian community. Back in the 60's and 70's many Pakistani men were being recruited by Manchester's textile Mills with promises of a better standard of life in the UK. While they no doubt had many things to adjust to in their newly adopted country; one thing they were unable to adjust to was the bland English food. So the first Curry Houses emerged to cater for the migrant Pakistani workers, *not* the English. Obviously those first Curry Houses were a lot different from the ones that have evolved and exist today, yet in Manchester you can still find authentic traditional Pakistani cooking being served up, such as you will find at Kabana in the City Centre. Kabana is still considered by many in the Manchester Pakistani community as 'one of the best'.

Kabana - Manchester City Centre   Kabana - Cheetham Hill

Something is changing!

It's over 22 years since I lived in Manchester but I have visited frequently over the years and on such a visit, a trip to the 'Curry Mile' was always a must! Sadly the last couple of years I have noticed some changes on the 'Curry Mile' that I fear may change its identity forever!

Many Shisha cafes, Arabic restaurants and falafel bars are now opening up on the 'Curry Mile' to cater for Manchester's growing Arab community. While I have nothing against this type of food myself, I still fear that these recent changes will change the original charm of the 'Curry Mile' and eventually it will change altogether. If Manchester's town planners don't halt the change the 'Curry Mile' might become known, in the not too distant future as, the 'Shisha Mile'!

Some people may argue; 'you can't halt progress...' and this is very true, nothing stays the same. However in my mind the 'Curry Mile' has always been unique and has always had that somewhat 'other world' feeling about it. Whenever we have taken friends there, they make comments like; "they feel like they have stepped into little Pakistan..."

The Manchester curry scene will no doubt survive and keep evolving just as the rest of BIR world does, but for me, call it nostalgia, there will always be - 'The Mancunian Way'.

Chapter 2

Back on the Curry Trail...

*"It is good to have an end to journey toward; but it
is the journey that matters, in the end."*
— Ernest Hemingway

I love that quote because is expresses a profound truth and one that applies to what I like to refer to as the 'Curry Trail'. Some people write books with titles and descriptions like, 'the definitive guide...' or the 'complete story...' however in the cooking world, and this most certainly applies to curry - there is <u>no such thing</u>! There is no definitive guide or no one book that tells the *complete* story. Why not? It's because this is an ever unfolding story!

Most readers of this book who know a little about the British Indian Restaurant {BIR} story will appreciate what I am talking about and if you have already bought my first e-book then you will understand where I am coming from with this.

Personally, I consider myself a perpetual student, when it comes to BIR cuisine and I never tire of the 'trail'. I certainly don't claim to know it all and I love nothing better than when someone e-mails me with a variation to a recipe in my book that he or she has experimented with and then discovered a new taste or characteristic; believe it or not, I have found in my own personal experience that the smallest of changes when cooking a curry can produce the most amazing variation or improvement.

There are many other Curry enthusiasts who like me have managed to get behind the kitchen door of their local 'Indian' restaurant and find out how things are done and they, like me have shared that knowledge with others, so read their books too!

Another thing; many names for curries on a lot of Restaurant or Takeaway menus are simply pure invention! I know that many of you will already know this, but I mention this because I constantly receive requests like; "how do you make a Special Chicken Balti Shakshuk..." {I made that up by the way - see how easy it is!} and I have to reply by saying; "I have never heard of it!"

'The secret to <u>that</u> Takeaway Curry Taste PART 1', the title of my first book and now Part 2 - is granted, a bit misleading because it almost implies that this cuisine that has come to be known as 'British Indian Restaurant' {BIR} can be defined so succinctly, whereas in actual fact the pursuit is a never ending one!

When I get e-mails saying; "I was told the way to make Onion Bhajis is this way..." or someone says, "that's not like the Chicken Jafflon I had at my local takeaway - which is the right way?" I always sigh slightly and then remind them that there is <u>no such thing</u> as a 'one right way' or a 'Governing Body for Curry.' What we have is a system that was devised and invented largely by the Bengali community here in the UK back in the 1960s and from that, there have come to be some commonly accepted ideas and practices along with a million and one variations all producing different, interesting and equally valid results.

My first e-book revealed to you most of that 'devised system' with some variations that I had learned from different Bengali & Indian Chefs and some I had come up with on my own; hence I named the book; *'The secret to <u>that</u> Takeaway Curry Taste PART 1'* the *secret* bit being the system of exactly how Indian Restaurants & Takeaways cook the curry we Brits' have come to know and love.

{If you haven't yet got that book I would really encourage you to get it as it lays the foundation on which this book will build}

Get it here: <u>http://goo.gl/0TWpW3</u>

Hopefully you will have bought the first e-book and so will be used to making the Base Gravies, Garlic & Ginger Paste, Tikka Masala Sauce, etc. In this book we will explore those things a little more, however there will be more focus on the British Indian Restaurant Takeaway Menu and the, *many many* curries, that perplex us when we struggle to decide what to have for our Friday night treat! You will learn recipes to many more Restaurant & Takeaway curries and yes, a few variations of our own.

For example, what's the connection between Chicken Malayan and Chicken Kashmir? You'll discover that in many cases the thing that separates one curry from another on the takeaway Menu is just one ingredient and yet, the amazing thing about that is, that *one* ingredient changes the taste and characteristic of the curry altogether!

This book will satisfy those who are curious to know how a Bengali or Pakistani Chef does it. Often many Asian BIR Chefs are reluctant to give away their own unique *secrets, tips* and recipes, yet in this book you will find that they do.

We will help you create your own BIR 'Home Curry Kitchen' by translating, if you will, how to cook BIR style curry at home without all the professional cookware and gadgets of a commercial kitchen. We will help by converting some of the recipes in this book to 2-4 portions as opposed to Base Gravy for 60 portions that you don't have the room in your freezer for! We will give you a 'Curry Chef's must have grocery list that will make sure you have all the spices, condiments and pickles in order to create a shed load of curries!

This book will also include the interesting story of another English bloke who being fanatical about curry took it to the next level and opened his own 'Indian Takeaway' and that he was inspired to do all that from learning about my story! I can't help but wonder, who is next?

You will also read about his own unique learning curve and insights into the Curry World.

So, here we are 'back on the trail' and it's my sincere wish that after reading *'The secret to <u>that</u> Takeaway Curry Taste PART 2'* that you will be a little further along that trail, but remember for the *real* curry lovers there is not an ultimate destination just an amazing onward journey!

So first, let's meet Adey Payne.

Chapter 3

Adey Payne & Curried Away

The 'Curried Away' Team 2013

How would I describe Adey? Well, he's a big bloke with a big heart! The first time I met Adey face-to-face, he gave me a big bear hug! I knew then, that we were going to get on just great!

When you talk to Adey, his passion and love for curry & cooking just oozes out of him! He also truly lives it; and when I say "lives it", I mean lives it! He is the only English Curry Chef I know who works Bengali hours; what I mean by that is that Bengali Chefs are famous for their incredible work ethic! It's nothing unusual for a typical Bengali Chef to work 80-100 hours a week and in one of the most pressured environment there is!

Well, Adey does just that! Curried Away is open seven days a week, eight hours a day and Adey is present for all of those hours, add to that, he does the buying from the cash & carry and runs a cooking class on a Sunday morning too! When I asked him how he coped, he just smiled and said; "I thrive on it Julian"!

Even though Adey is the owner and Head Chef at Curried Away he has at least two other Curry Chef's under him, Danny and Sultan. The problem is that Adey cannot rest unless he himself is at the helm making sure everything that leaves Curried Away is nothing less than perfect!

To give you an example of this, when I first entered Adey's realm - his Kitchen, it was lunchtime on a Tuesday afternoon; Curried Away serves a traditional English menu in the day time, breakfasts and lunches that sort of thing. Well, this Tuesday afternoon he had taken an order for a cooked English breakfast and Danny, one of his other Chefs was in the process of cooking this while Adey and I were chatting about curry.

I couldn't help notice while we were talking 'Curry' that Adey seemed somewhat distracted from our conversation by the way Danny was cooking the mushrooms to accompany the cooked breakfast. Suddenly, Adey grabbed the helm from Danny, put his mushrooms in the bin and made some fresh ones - he then went on to relate to me with great enthusiasm about the way English people like their mushrooms cooked and how he has applied this method to his Mushroom fried rice recipe. "Wow!" I thought; someone as crackers as me!

To be honest, you have to be a bit like that to succeed in the Food game. We have become a nation of food critics with very high standards and if you operate a food business you have to be prepared to go that extra mile and put passion and flare into your food or you simply will not rise above the competition. Adey certainly does that! As of the time of writing this Curried Away got voted Number 1 on Trip Advisor for eating out in Boston. Check it out here: http://goo.gl/9Pu0jF

Adey discloses to me that he had spent, like me, over 20 years seeking out the ingredients and methods to real BIR style curry! The fact that Adey, very kindly, openly acknowledges that he made great strides in his journey because of my videos on YouTube and my first e-book, is one of those things that makes my own personal struggle in cracking the 'curry code' very worthwhile and of course, I am flattered by how he credits me with a lot of what he has learned.

Adey relates to me, as we chat over a cup of coffee, about his various experiences in the cooking world that led up to him being able to realise his dream of becoming a 'Curry Chef' and opening his own outlet.

There have been Burger vans, a stint as a head Chef in a prison etc... "Prison! Were you working there...?"? I asked.

The Four-armed Chef?

"No, I was an inmate".

He smiles looking a little embarrassed, then relates that he was only in Prison for a few months and that because of his good behaviour they put him in charge of the kitchen!

"Any 'Curry Nights' in prison?", "No". he laughs.

Adey is a man of many passions and talents one of which is his music. Adey has been in many a band and describes himself as a "Guitar Slag".

Something that impressed me about Adey when I first met him was his honesty. Adey tells it like it is and expects everyone around him to do the same. When I first tried one of his curries, he said; "I want you to be completely honest with me... and I mean completely honest"! How could I be anything less than that?

However, having tried his curry, I had to say; "superb"! I can honestly say that I have rarely tasted a curry as tasty and as well balanced in many an Indian Restaurant that I have eaten in {and believe me, I have eaten in many!} as the first curry Adey served me.

Adey refuses to take all the credit. In keeping with his insistence on honesty he insists on giving due credit to his former Head Chef Abdul whom he refers to as a, "Master Chef..." and like "Family..."

He also gives a lot of credit to Danny his assistant Chef who, in Adey's estimation has learned the ropes of "cooking in a curry Kitchen incredibly fast"!

He also refers to Danny as his "Guinea Pig" in that he makes Danny try all his experimentations first, to gauge his reaction, including Adey's infamous 'Jhalzala Curry' devised and created by Adey to be the world's hottest curry and judging by Danny's reaction in front of me as Adey thrusts a spoon in Danny's direction insisting Danny takes a "… good mouthful." I don't doubt that it is probably the world's hottest curry; in fact I couldn't resist trying it myself and it was probably one of the hottest curries I had ever tried!

There is something in Adey's relationship with Danny that reminds me of the Muppets Show's 'Beaker' – Doctor Bunsen's trusted side kick who was forever the unwilling victim of Doctor Bunsen's experiments!

While Danny is quietly choking in the corner of the kitchen from Jhalzala exposure, Adey casts an affectionate eye over to his trusted helper to check he hasn't stopped breathing.

If you're not a child of the seventies then you might not be familiar with Doctor Bunsen and Beaker from the Muppet Show. Here is a link:
https://youtu.be/EFebGZ7FJQQ

Then there's Debbie; she is front of house. I notice her paying particularly close attention to details as we are served our first curry at Curried Away and I can't help but be impressed by how immaculately clean everything appears.

Later on I cast a glance at Debbie as she stands quietly in the corner of the kitchen absorbing the goings on as a few well-chosen swear words fly across the kitchen. I glance at Debbie who seems impervious to the mayhem and just smiles with raised eyebrows. It's obvious she has become well accustomed to it all.

Adey relates, that on a Friday and Saturday night when they are at their busiest; "the air can turn quite blue!" He relates than many a customer who is stood just the other side of the kitchen door, howls with laughter at what they can hear coming from the other side! It's probably come to be part of their regular Friday night's entertainment.

After we said goodbye late Tuesday night after spending the whole day with Adey and the team at Curried Away; I felt we had made some good friends and my overall impression of Adey was that, yes he was a bit of a rough diamond, but essentially a really genuine and nice bloke! I knew then that having made the decision to include Adey & Curried Away in my new venture - 'The *secret* to that Takeaway Curry Taste PART 2' - I had made the right choice!

So let's get cooking!

Chapter 4

Tips & Tricks for Restaurant like Results!

'...The 'Base' is just a base...'

I get a number e-mails from people who have been trying to cook BIR style curry for years but still can't seem to achieve the right taste.

They have followed numerous Base Gravy recipes, tried different ingredients but still that taste eludes them. Many people still hold the belief that they are missing a 'vital ingredient.'

What I point out every time and this usually works, is that the problem is generally the same - it's _how_ they are cooking it, not necessarily *what* they are cooking. The Base is just a base, as the word 'base' suggests, it needs building on.

Many cooks gets too hung up on ingredients while at the same time forgetting the other just as vital half of the equation - *techniques!*

Many mistakenly believe that if they discover the "right" Base Gravy recipe they will crack 'that taste'! This is NOT true. I have related the experience of a guy who came to visit me at 'Curry 2 Go' in Chorley all the way from Birmingham and told me that he was so frustrated with his own curry cooking results that he came to the conclusion it must be the Base Gravy he was making that was wrong. So guess what he did? He talked his local 'Indian' takeaway owner into selling him a batch of *their* Base gravy and he hurriedly went back home to cook with it!

Guess what the results were? That's right - no difference! I demonstrated to him on that busy Saturday he visited me, exactly how you cook the Base {any base!} right.

I have often found when I have been teaching someone to cook curry that what I often observe is their preoccupation with the *ingredients and amounts* - for example, I have often observed, while a student is fussing over whether his Chef's spoon has a few too many grains of spice content on it, that they are completely unaware of the smell of burning coming from the Garlic & Ginger Paste frying in the pan. They then wonder why the resulting curry doesn't taste right.

The answer is simple. They need to pay attention to each and every step in the process and make sure that each step is *right*. You need to practice slowly using a lower heat at first until you feel confident with your cooking, then when you get more confident turn up the heat and do it quicker like they do in the 'Indian' Restaurants and Takeaways.

It will make very little observable difference if you add in quarter of a teaspoon too much Tandoori Masala or half a teaspoon too little of Garlic & Ginger Paste but what will make a huge discernible difference is how you cook those spices, Garlic and Ginger etc...

What I have noticed over the years of cooking curry for a living, was that some of the best curries I have made, have often been made when I have been mad busy rather than quiet. Why is that?

Well when you're busy, you are 'on a roll' - as they say, and your cooking technique has become almost instinctive and you are very much using your 'right brain' which is said to be your intuitive side.

To illustrate this, when you first start learning to drive, every function you perform - engage gear, check your mirror, control your clutch {all at the same time!} - all feel unnatural and awkward and you wonder how you will ever get to drive without *this* feeling as well as constantly making mistakes; but you do!

The way we move from awkwardness to naturalness in the kitchen is simply by the process of repetition. When it comes to cooking curry - it is exactly the same!

Obviously until you get to that point it can be very frustrating getting results that are a bit hit and miss, so I am going to give you the benefit of my experience in analysing some of the various cooking techniques, ingredients, timings and common mistakes, so as to give you a head start. This chapter will also include some quick fixes and tricks used by Chefs in 'Indian' restaurants, so let's take a peep behind the kitchen door and see how it's done.

Oil Temperature

The starting point of cooking any curry starts with heating the oil in the pan, yet this {if you are not careful} is where it can all go wrong!

If the oil is not hot enough when you add the Garlic & Ginger Paste and then the rest of the ingredients you will kill the dish! The oil must be hot enough, here's why:

The oil regulates your pan temperature - in other words your cooking temperature. If the oil in the pan is cold or simply not hot enough, then the first thing that will happen is the Garlic & Ginger Paste will not cook out, and if it doesn't cook then the taste of the resulting curry will taste of raw garlic which is very different from cooked garlic, not to mention the raw ginger.

Raw spices. In many of my videos as well as in my first book I mention the importance of 'cooking out the spices.' This technique simply refers to drawing out the volatile oils from the spices - which are where the flavour and aroma come from.

If the oil in the pan is not hot enough then this doesn't happen and the resulting curry will taste flat. Also, raw spices can make the curry taste bitter. If your house doesn't smell like an 'Indian' when you are cooking your curry, then your curry won't taste like an 'Indian' when you are eating it! Does that make sense? Be <u>careful</u> not to burn the spices too as this will kill the curry!

When it comes to cooking spices, often we can cook them longer than we might realise. For example if your spices are being cooked in oil only, at a high temperature the chances are that you will probably burn them. However, if you add the spices after you have added the tomato paste you can push them harder for longer, before adding the first ladle of Base Gravy. In the case of non-tomato based curries like Garlic Chicken, then add just about a Chef's spoon of Base Gravy to prolong the cook time of the spices - this will ensure you draw out the maximum flavour from the spices and this will off course result in tastier curries!

<u>Tomato Paste</u>. Most curries are made with a tomato base which provides the sweet, almost tart taste, that gives curries like Madras that characteristic flavour and depth. Tomatoes are acidic by nature and the taste of raw tomatoes as opposed to thoose cooked is markedly different. When you cook a sugar containing food {like tomatoes} they caramelise and the sugar content in the food gives a different taste to the dish. This happens with tomatoes and tomato paste in a curry. If the oil in your pan is not hot enough, then the tomato paste will not release those compound sugars. Also, you will be left with an overly acidic or overly tart taste in the curry, which doesn't balance with other tastes - this too can kill your curry!

The Italians understand this principle well. Have you ever enjoyed a really tasty Marinara sauce or Bolognaise from an authentic Italian restaurant? The tomato sauce has a smooth rich flavour that almost has a molasses overtone from the caramelised sugars in the tomatoes. You can detect that *same* rich flavour from a Madras or Vindaloo that has been cooked well. That is why those two curries are very satisfying, I am sure you know what I mean.

Pre-Cooked Meat

A word about pre-cooked meat. The cold pre-cooked meat needs to reach cooking temperature as quickly as possible for two reasons. First is safety; you need to know that before you serve the curry - that the meat in it has been heated through and is therefore safe. The second reason is that you want that meat or fish to take on the flavour of that curry - in other words to taste like the two have been cooked together for hours. The high cooking temperatures in the 'Curry pan' {another reason why aluminium pans are superior} cause the meat fibres to open and absorb the sauce and spices, which does not happen if the pan is not hot enough!

Roasting

Roasting is a technique I mention in one of my first videos on YouTube which discusses the benefits of Aluminium pans and why they are used. If you are not cooking with a high enough temperature then *this* process doesn't happen. Believe it or not this alone is *the* most common mistake made by many a new Curry Chef. The idea is simple, the base that you need to 'roast' {or caramelise} is made up of what principle ingredient? Onions. What do onions contain that create that irresistible curry yumminess? Sugar! How are these sugar compounds released? By heat. If you don't get this bit right your curry will taste 'soupy' and lack that lip smacking quality. Does this make sense?

How do you make sure that you are employing this technique correctly? Here are some tips:

Make sure the pan temperature is hot enough before adding any Base Gravy - you will know if the Tomato Paste is bubbling fairly vigorously and you will smell the spices releasing their volatile oils.

2 Appearance. The appearance of the curry will change. It should start to look glossy, which happens once the Base is caramelised sufficiently. This is the caramelised sugar that gives it this appearance.

3 Add only a small quantity of Base Gravy at a time, I recommend about ½ - ¾ of a ladle (about 100ml) this will ensure the pan temperature isn't cooled too much and the 'roasting' time {caramelising} is shorter. Here are some pointers that will indicate that the small quantity of Base is caramelised sufficiently. Thickness - you should be aiming at reducing the volume by at least a third. Oiling - once cooked sufficiently the base will separate from the oil, you will see it rising to the top - this indicates it's time to add more gravy. Smell - once you become an 'instinctive cook' your senses would heighten and you'll start to observe details, perhaps not discerned before, like different smells. Once cooked {or caramelised} the base will smell sweeter. Don't panic if you are unable to discern this straight away because if you are in a state of *over concentration,* in other words slightly panicky, then you will not notice the smell. This may take some time to acquire. It took me over 12 months of cooking curries for a living to pick up on these subtle changes; years of practice before I had started 'Curry 2 Go' never got me there!

Pots, Pans etc...
{try http://www.genware.co.uk}

I have already mentioned in my previous book and on other Youtube videos that Aluminium pans are the Chefs choice in an Indian Restaurant or Takeaway due to the excellent heat conducting ability. If you can't source Aluminium pans {I know they are difficult to find} then opt for a black Iron pan or even a stainless steel pan. As mentioned above, the 'Roasting' technique helps caramelise the sugars from the onions and tomatoes and thus creates that lip smacking yummy taste that characterises good BIR food. Non-stick pans will **NOT** allow you to caramelise the sauce and sugars in the food, thus the resulting dish will end up tasting like there is something missing.

I also recommend getting a professional stainless steel Chef's spoon to compliment the Aluminium pan, this enables you then to scrape off the residue or caramelised sauce. A wooden or plastic spoon wouldn't do that and you would end up with a brown or black like residue stuck to the bottom of the pan once the curry is cooked. It would not just make the washer upper annoyed but would also mean you have not managed to scrape off those tasty caramelised bits into the curry.

Seasoning

Under or over seasoning any dish will kill it! Believe it or not this simple mistake of not getting the seasoning right is a common problem for any inexperienced Chef and even a few experienced ones! If you have ever watched Gordon Ramsay's Kitchen Nightmares, then you will no doubt notice that this simple thing is something that Gordon constantly points out as a major reason as to why the food lets a particular restaurant down. In most cases the problem is underseasoning.

This issue is even more critical when it comes to curry cooking. Any Curry served underseasoned will taste bland, no matter how many spices you put in it! In fact, try it, make a curry and deliberately put in a third of the usual amount of salt and taste it. You wouldn't believe how this small mistake can undo all the other great work you have done - getting the Base Gravy right, the spices cooked just right, the meat all nicely marinated and cooked to perfection, then just by missing out the salt or not adding enough - you kill the dish! I think what this illustrates is simply, what great cooking is, that it's many little things that make the whole and if you miss out one of those little things you don't get the results you are looking for. Does this make sense?

In my first book I made the comment that anyone can be a great curry Chef, and that's true, but the first thing any Chef has to know is this - what the finished dish is *supposed* to taste like. You have to have that *taste as it were* in your mind as the starting point. The best way to acquire this ability is to eat the dish you are seeking to re-create often! Analyse the tastes in the dish, the texture - the seasoning!

Obviously, the most common mistake in cooking is under seasoning, but over seasoning is a concern too and obviously less correctable! If you find you can't trust your own palate when it comes to seasoning, then why not ask someone else to taste it and get their opinion. Sometimes when we have been sampling too many things you can lose your palate.

If the curry or dish you are cooking includes onions, either sliced or diced, add your salt in at this stage as it will help prevent your onions from burning and aides them in turning soft.

> **Adey's Tip.** Just as lemon is used to help reduce the heat if you have accidentally put in too much chilli powder, Adey assures me this trick works the same if you put in too much salt. *It might not help your husband or wife's blood pressure though!*

Another important consideration is the temperature you serve your food. I have found that in this country we often serve our food too hot. I think this has obviously come about because we live many months of the year in a cold climate and we often try to compensate for that by eating our food piping hot!

I noticed when living in the Canaries that the Canarians don't eat their food piping hot as most cultures from warmer climates. This is also true in South Asian cuisine; they serve their food warm to hot. This is important because, how much of the food can we taste if it's too hot? Not much. We desensitize our taste buds when we eat food too hot.

To prove this point - have you ever had a leftover curry in the fridge and the next morning when you open the fridge to make your breakfast you catch a whiff of last night's curry and you can't resist grabbing a mouthful? How does it taste? Fantastic! In fact doesn't it taste better than when you had it the night before? Obviously the curry has had the chance to marinate in the fridge over night, but really the reason that the curry now tastes *so good* is that it's cold and your taste buds are more able to pick out all those subtle flavours from the spices better than when you ate it hot. Does this make sense?

So, the point you need to take from this is not to serve or eat your curries too hot if you really want to appreciate all those flavours.

The Use of Condiments

British Indian Restaurant & Takeaway style cooking is all about speed and being able to infuse intense flavours into dishes fast!

One way this is achieved is by the use of condiments. You will be amazed how by just adding a teaspoon of a particular condiment you can create fantastic flavours as well as a whole new dish!

Here is a list of condiments commonly used in the BIR kitchen and a description of how these condiments are used.

Garlic Pickle

This brand is a very popular one and commonly used in many BIR kitchens. Another popular brand if you can't source this one is the National brand; I have used both and found them excellent.

Garlic Pickle is used in so many dishes to add intense flavours. I couldn't list them all but here are some popular dishes that feature this pickle, and don't forget to experiment yourself!

Garlic Chilli Chicken. This pickle is added to the hot oil just after the Garlic & Ginger paste and before fresh sliced garlic goes into the pan. Not only does this pickle add that extra dimension of Garlic to this particular dish, but the pickling spices that have been marinating for months in the oil of the pickle add an incredible layer of flavour too.

Just add 1 heaped tsp or less. Don't be tempted to add more otherwise you will overpower the dish and ruin it. A takeaway local to where I live does this and I have to remind the Chef every time I order a curry from them to go easy on the pickle!

Jalfrezi. Garlic Pickle works really well in this dish and can be added into the hot oil after the peppers and chillies have been fried off slightly. Again about a tsp or less will do. {*For this recipe, see 'The secret to <u>that</u> Takeaway Curry Taste PART 1'*}

Lamb Achari. This dish is traditionally made with pickling spices or the short cut version in the BIR kitchen is with the use of Lime Pickle. Try adding just ½ a tsp to the hot oil after the Garlic & Ginger Paste. {*For this recipe, see 'The secret to <u>that</u> Takeaway Curry Taste PART 1'*}

Mr Naga. Try adding just ½ a tsp to this curry about the same time you add the Mr Naga Pickle. {see Chapter 6 for this recipe}

Tamarind Sauce

Tamarind Sauce or 'Tamarina' as this brand calls it is a real taste of India! Where do you think HP or Brown sauce {aka Wilson's Gravy} got its influence from? Britain's colonial adventure in India influenced the food we now think of as traditional 'English.' If you have ever eaten *real* Indian food, particularly the Vegetarian variety, you will have come across this tart but tasty condiment usually served up with Chaat or vegetable samosas. Some BIR Chefs I have known actually just use HP or Brown sauce in their dishes, but personally I find the Tamarina sauce by Maggi to be the best as it's less acidic and has more of the Tamarind extract in it, whereas the HP and other Brown sauces have things like dates and molasses in them. However why not experiment with both.

This condiment is usually added into a dish during the final cooking stage so that it retains its tart characteristic. {*see the recipe Lamb Tamaria in Chapter 6*}

Other dishes this condiment works well in are sweet and sour dishes like Patia and Dhansak. Just add a heaped tsp towards the end of the cooking process. Of course this condiment works really well as a dip with samosas and Aloo Tikki.

Adey's Tip. Try adding a dash of Worcestershire sauce, also a Tamarind derived sauce, to a Chicken Dhansak towards the end for a great flavour.

Tomato Ketchup

"Surely not!" I hear you say. Yep, this is another condiment used in the BIR Kitchen to create delicious flavours as well as colour.

Dishes like Chasni utilise tomato ketchup. {see Chapter 6 for the recipe}

Other dishes that Tomato Ketchup works well in are Korai and Samber.

Adey's Tip. Add 2 TBSP of Tomato Ketchup to a Korai at mid cooking stage to add a subtle sweet flavour and amazing colours!

Tomato Ketchup is also added to dips that you might get with your poppadoms. Try this great tasting dip:

INGREDIENTS & METHOD – GREAT TASTING DIP

1. Heinz Tomato Ketchup (10 TBSP)
2. Lemon Juice (1 TBSP) {Fresh}
3. Methi Leaves (1 tsp) {Rub in your hands to make like a powder}
4. Chilli Powder (1 ~ 2 pinches)
5. Garam Masala (1 pinch)
6. Mango Chutney (1 TBSP)
7. Simply mix all the ingredients together well and preferably leave for a couple of hours before serving. Try with poppadoms.

Other dishes that I have known Tomato Ketchup added to are Chicken Tikka Masala, Dhansak, and Rogan Josh. Again why not experiment!

Chilli Pickle

This pickle is simply *magical* in its ability to create incredible flavour. The brand we use at 'Curry 2 Go' and the only one I recommend is Patak's. The reason I prefer this brand is the fact it has more chilli in it and a lot less oil.

Green chillies are used in South Asian cooking not just for the heat they provide to a dish but more for the flavour. If you add just half a tsp of this pickle to almost any spicy curry or side dish you will not believe the transformation. {See 'The secret to *that* Takeaway Curry Taste PART 1' for recipes}

This pickle is great as an accompaniment with any Dhal based curry. Often dhal based curries are sometimes quite bland or lacking intense flavours. Try serving some dhal, plain basmati rice, some raita and about a tablespoon amount of Patak's Chilli Pickle. Serve them up on a Thali {Indian compartmentalised plate} and you have got a great meal!

You can even use this versatile pickle with non-Asian dishes. Try a Jacob's cracker with some Wensleydale or a similar strong white cheese with a dollop of Patak's chilli pickle - *Yum!*

Mango Chutney

I have already covered the use of this condiment in Part 1 but I felt the need to re-iterate the fact that this condiment is likely the most used condiment of all! Not only is this condiment used in many a curry to add that subtle sweet background flavour but it is also used in Base Gravy recipes and dips, and is the magical ingredient in 'Red Onions'.

See recipe here: https://youtu.be/54wIreqDJ70

Mr Naga Pickle

Mr Naga Pickle is what inspired the curry dish - 'Mr Naga' This pickle like the Patak's Chilli Pickle also has magical abilities when it comes to transforming a dish and infusing flavour.

Naga chillies are also known as Bhut Jolokia and Ghost Chillies and are reputed to be amongst the hottest chillies in the world.

They also are used for their flavour. In BIR style curries ½ a tsp of Mr Naga Pickle will give an incredible fruity hot flavour to a curry. I use this in the 'Mr Naga' curry recipe in this book which is not particularly a mind blowingly hot curry but is rather a curry with a sweet characteristic and real depth of flavour. You will find that BIR Chefs add ½ a tsp of this condiment to almost any spicy curry like - Madras, Vindaloo, Jhafrezi, Southern Indian Chilli Chicken and many more. I have always been reticent about doing that because you can end up with all your curries just tasting the same.

Mr Naga Pickle works really well with fish & vegetable dishes and helps add a real depth of flavour to any bland dish.

Soy Sauce

OK, I know what you are thinking; "Is this an Indian or Chinese cook book?" Seriously, Dark Soy Sauce is used to add a rich flavour particularly to lamb or meat dishes. The recipe Lamb Naath in this book includes the use of Soy Sauce. A dash of Soy Sauce is added half way through the cooking process and will add more flavour than salt but, be careful to adjust additional Salting if using Soy Sauce.

Still not convinced it is used in BIR cooking? Ingredients used in BIR cooking:

  https://youtu.be/N_tkHyOzU8w

Mint Sauce

Used in everything from Tikka Masala Sauce to Pakistani Green Lamb curry as well as dips and sauces, this is a must have in the fridge for the BIR curry cooking enthusiast. In fact, one day I accidentally left this out of a batch of Tikka Masala Sauce I was making and I could not figure out why all the Chicken Tikka Masalas that I tasted that day, didn't taste quite right.

This condiment is a vital ingredient or taste in one of Britain's most loved curries - Chicken Tikka Masala.

Lime Pickle

Lime Pickle is best known as an accompaniment in the pickle tray with your poppadoms. This pickle really does wake up your taste buds! As I have already mentioned in Part 1, this pickle is used in Lamb Achari to help add that intense sour element. I have also used this pickle in Vindaloo which already has lime juice added. If you are using this in a curry like Vindaloo just add 1 tsp and make sure to mash it up into a paste so that it dissolves into the curry.

Balti Paste

Here is another condiment that has created a bit of controversy. Many can't accept that a ready-made curry paste that, let's face it, an amateur home curry Chef would likely use to make a curry is being used in Indian Restaurants and takeaways to make Balti dishes and other curries. This paste is used in the BIR kitchen because it is made from primarily onions and Garam spices {depending on the brand used}. I can honestly say I have never seen any other curry paste {like Vindaloo}, this paste is used in many curry dishes from Balti to Moghul and it just adds a richness that Balti and dishes like Moghul are known for. Some 'purists' don't like the thought of using ready-made pastes from a jar but remember, in the BIR kitchen three things are important: {1} Speed, {2} Cost, and {3} Results, and the use of pastes and other condiments help achieve those objectives.

Years ago, restaurants made their own Balti Paste {some still do}. Here is my recipe, it will keep in the fridge for 2 weeks:

INGREDIENTS – HOMEMADE BALTI PASTE

1. Onions (6) {Large, roughly chopped}
2. Vegetable Oil (300 ml)
3. Green Chillies (4)
4. Tomatoes (2) {medium}
5. Garam Masala (2 TBSP)
6. Coriander Seeds (1 TBSP) {freshly ground}
7. Garlic Bulb (1) {Whole bulb, peeled and roughly chopped}
8. Ginger (5cm piece) {Root, finely chopped}
9. Salt (1 tsp)
10. Turmeric (1 tsp)
11. Cumin Seeds (1 TBSP) {freshly ground}
12. Star Anise (1)
13. Bay Leaves (2) {Asian}
14. Cinnamon (2) {Stick cinnamon}
15. Tomato Purée (1 TBSP) {Good quality}
16. Water (200 ml)

METHOD – HOMEMADE BALTI PASTE

1. Heat the oil in a large 3 litre pan
2. Once hot add the star anise, cinnamon and bay leaves and fry for 2 minutes.
3. Next, add all the powdered spices and salt and cook out for 2 minutes.
4. Now add the Garlic, Ginger and Green chillies and tomatoes, cook for 1-2 minutes.
5. Next add the tomato purée and cook for 1 minute.
6. Now, add the onions and mix well with the oil and spice mixture.
7. Once the onions begin to soften slightly add the 200 ml of water, bring back to a simmer and put the pan lid on, turn down the heat to low and cook the mixture for 20 minutes. Check occasionally to make sure the mixture isn't too dry and thus ends up burning. If it is too dry, just add a little more water.
8. After 20 minutes the onions should be almost dissolved and you should have your onion paste. If the onions are not cooked enough, cook for a little longer.
9. Once done, remove the star anise, cinnamon stick and bay leaves, allow the mixture to cool completely and leave at least for 24 hours before use. Add 1 H/TBSP to any curry you like and you will have a sauce that has a real depth of flavour.
10. This is what they used to use years ago particularly in the 1980 to create curries like we used to have.

There's nothing worse than burnt garlic!

Having spent some time discussing how important it is to cook with the pan hot enough, I also need to mention the importance of not having it too hot! Nothing illustrates the validity of this point more than burnt garlic! If you have cooked many a curry then I am sure that you, like me have fallen foul of this mistake. I cannot count the amount of times on a busy Saturday afternoon I have had to bin a curry because I had burnt the garlic - too many I can tell you!

I am sure if this has happened to you too you will appreciate what I mean when I say, "there's nothing worse than burnt garlic..." In a way, the garlic in the pan acts a bit like a barometer on your heat level - if the garlic burns then the heats too high!

What may be worse is not realising that you have actually burnt the garlic!

Some things to look for and this applies both to Garlic & Ginger Paste and sliced garlic such as that used in 'Garlic Chilli Chicken.'

5 | Buy Garlic that is firm, not spongy and if possible the bigger the individual cloves the better.

6 | Do <u>NOT</u> keep it in the fridge. Garlic needs to breathe so do not keep it in a plastic bag. The best place is to keep it on the windowsill in a bowl but preferably out of sunlight.

7 | The finer the garlic is made into a paste the more potent its flavour enhancing power become.

8 To remove the smell of Garlic from your hands rub them with a little salt and lemon juice, then rinse in cold water; works a treat!

9 If you want to create a dish with a strong flavour of garlic, add it raw towards the end of the cooking of the dish. A Pakistani Chef showed me this trick and it works a treat!

Do <u>NOT</u> brown the garlic! With the exception of one or two dishes, you really don't want to be browning the garlic. Once you allow the garlic in the pan to turn brown it loses its flavour and acquires a whole different type of flavour.

When you are adding your Garlic & Ginger Paste to the hot oil in the pan, listen for the sizzle {which is the water content in the paste} as soon as it diminishes - then straight in with the other ingredients this will ensure the garlic doesn't burn.

When you make a batch of Garlic & Ginger Paste you can add a little water to buy you a little time in the cooking process and prevent the Garlic from prematurely burning. Adey only uses Garlic Paste in many of his curries and this is how he makes it:

Adey's Garlic Paste

 https://youtu.be/6zOb9ebJi3g

Once you have mastered getting your pan to just the right cooking temperature you are well on your way to creating some tasty curries and limiting your mistakes.

One question I get asked a lot is, which is better, cooking with Gas or Electric? The answer is Gas. That doesn't mean that you can't get tasty results with an electric hob, the benefits of Gas are better heat regulation and speed of temperature reduction or increase and the flaming effect.

Flaming

How many of us have stood watching in awe as we see a Chef cooking our curry perhaps in an open plan kitchen and suddenly - whoosh the flames catch the contents of the pan and it appears that the food in the pan is on fire!

Actually it is! The reason this happens is that the oil in the pan, once it reaches a certain temperature, becomes volatile and once that volatile hot oil touches a naked flame it combusts.

Does this add any beneficial flavour or is it merely a bit of theatre? Well, the answer is both. Flaming or as the French say Flambé {however the flambé technique usually involves alcohol whereas in BIR cooking it doesn't}. Many doubt that 'flaming' is anything more than just a bit of theatre.

Flaming in the BIR kitchen is not really a necessary cooking technique employed in order to achieve a vital flavour or characteristic. It simply happens because Chefs cook at high temperatures and with oil and the two combined result in combustion. In fact in a busy BIR kitchen it can sometimes become a bit of a nuisance when you are mad busy with 4 or 5 curries on the go and you're having to fight fires!

Having said all of that, it is true that with a number of dishes the flaming technique adds a certain charred taste that compliments the dish, here are some dishes that benefit from flaming:

Any spinach based dish like Saag Aloo. The spinach in Saag Aloo is quite bland in taste and watery in texture too, so in order to get flavour into this dish it is generally dry fried on a high flame. This has the effect of caramelising the sugars thus intensifying the flavours {'Roasting'}. However, if you employ the flaming technique with this dish it really does benefit from that slightly smoky taste. Here is how you do it:

First heat the pan on a moderate to high flame. Next add in the oil. Once the oil is hot {will take about 1 minute} add the Garlic & Ginger Paste and take the pan off the heat so as to ensure you don't burn the Garlic. Add the tomato paste and spices, and put them back on the heat. Get the mixture to a vigorous simmer then add in the spinach and push the whole mixture with the back of the Chef's spoon around the pan, particularly to the edge or the rim to ensure it touches the flame and - whoosh it should catch fire! Allow the mixture to burn for no longer than about 3 seconds that is all that's needed. To stop the flames just remove the pan from the heat.

Another dish that benefits from Flaming is Chicken Tikka Masala. Believe it or not this sweet and creamy dish tastes great when the Chef has 'flamed' it.

There aren't many BIR Chefs I know that get this right but some of the best Bengali restaurants I have visited get it right with this dish. The High sugar content in this dish means that when you allow the sauce to ignite for a few seconds the caramelised or burnt sugars create an almost treacle like flavour that along with the Tandoor or Chargrilled chicken works so well! I am not particularly a fan of Chicken Tikka Masala, but if it's cooked right as I have just described and with a bit of added Jhal {fresh chillies} then I can quite enjoy this curry.

Use Fresh Ingredients

This is an obvious one but I would like to emphasise the importance of fresh ingredients. As foods age they not only look inferior than their fresh counterparts but also taste inferior too. I don't know about you but I have eaten in one too many a restaurant that has served up 'old food' and it tastes bland. They obviously do this in an effort to cut costs and they generally do that because they are not busy, and they are not busy because the food doesn't taste great - it's a vicious circle.

At 'Curry 2 Go' we don't compromise when it comes to fresh produce and the results speak for themselves because our customers often comment on the freshness and taste of our food and Adey also stipulates that only fresh ingredients go into his curries and dishes.

Certain items can be frozen for use and convenience but here I will provide you with a list of things you might want to keep your eye on.

Spices

Even though spices are dried, they do have a shelf life. Spices contain 'essential oils' that over time lose their potency. I recommend keeping your powdered spices no longer than 6 months and keep them in an air tight container out of direct sunlight. Chilli powder loses its red colour if kept for too long. A simple test to know if your spices are still fresh is to smell them. If the aroma isn't very strong then they have passed their best.

Whole spices can be kept for up to 2 years so generally no worries there. Why not grind you own spices for that extra flavour that you will undoubtedly get. I know a Pakistani Chef that always grinds Coriander and Cumin fresh and you can really tell the difference. This is something we copied at 'Curry 2 Go' and the difference was remarkable!

Vegetables

The two most important vegetable in Curry are tomatoes {I *know*, they are a fruit} and onions. I have a pet hate for those pale rock hard tasteless tomatoes so often found at many of the big supermarkets. One reason they are tasteless is that they aren't ripe! If you have a choice between a tomato that is pale red or orange in colour, rock hard and blemish free or a deep red tomato that is a bit squashy with the odd dimple here and there - choose that one!

The same applies to other veggies like peppers. Those rock hard and tasteless pale green or pale red peppers lack flavour and I avoid them, what I look for is a pepper that is dark green or red and just starting to turn a little bit soft - these ones taste great and infuse flavour into any dish! In fact try mixing some finely diced green or red pepper in with any spicy curry for an added depth of flavour.

You might wonder where you might find these squashy tomatoes or slightly soft peppers, the answer is Asian stores. The big supermarkets follow of policy of where all fruit and veg has to look like it has just come of a production line rather than grown from the soil or just picked from a tree, I am sure you know what I mean - tomatoes have to be a certain size and shape and all that stuff. In the

Asian {south Asian} stores they know their customers don't care if a tomato has a dimple or a pepper is an odd shape, as long as it tastes good!

In India and Bangladesh, tomatoes form the base for many curries but Bengali Chef's on arriving in the UK in the early 60's started adding tomato purée because British grown tomatoes simply didn't have enough of a *tomato* flavour. In fact, there is a small Indian restaurant {*real* Indian restaurant} in Manchester that makes their tomato paste from over ripe tomatoes and the results are superb, honestly this restaurant makes the best Madras I have ever tasted!

Onions also develop a more intense flavour as they dry out a little after picking and as most onions in the UK are imported they usually are just about right when they land in the shops. Obviously make sure the onions are not too old which you will be able to tell by the feel; they should be firm not spongy. BIR restaurant's generally use the Dutch variety which are sweeter than Spanish or English onions.

Here is a little tip for you; peeled, whole, sliced or chopped onions that have been left a few hours before being used in cooking develop a stronger flavour and this is why many BIR restaurants peel the onions for tomorrow's batch of Gravy the night before and just leave them in the pot ready for cooking the next day.

Veggies like okra, aubergine, mushrooms {I know they aren't a vegetable!}, carrots and cauliflower are all best if fresh. Many BIR takeaways and some restaurants use frozen mixed veg bags but the results in my opinion are poor. This is one of the first things I ask when visiting a new 'Indian' restaurant and if they use frozen veggies I don't stay.

Having ranted on about fresh and frozen vegetables I do make an exception to the rule and that is spinach. In my opinion spinach freezes really well and there is little discernible difference between fresh or frozen, not to mention how convenient it is to use frozen particularly when running a busy kitchen.

Fresh coriander is a must, but getting your hands on this out of season {Nov - Mar} can be a challenge, even from the Asian Cash & Carrys. One tip I learnt for extending the shelf life of coriander is to put it in brown paper bags in a cupboard *not* the fridge - we do this at 'Curry 2 Go' and we can get a week or longer out of our coriander. Don't forget to use the stalks chopped to add that extra flavour to a dish.

Adey's Magic Vegetables

 https://youtu.be/4I4sG6QzkFI

Many of us who are familiar with the pre-cooking of onions {Onions Sauce} pre-cooked peppers and onions {added to Balti & Bhuna recipes} know this is a very common way of quickly preparing dishes and adding flavours and textures. Adey and Curried Away do things a little differently watch the video above for 'Adey's Magic Vegetables' his method gets great results!

Fresh Meat

While meat in the BIR restaurant or takeaway is generally pre-cooked to save time it's often employed to save money too. Pre-cooked meat will keep in the fridge for 3 days. However if you leave it longer than that it loses its flavour and quality. Frozen pre-cooked meat I don't recommend. I have tried it in an effort to save a few quid but I noticed the meat once thawed became quite stringy so I dropped that pretty quick.

Fresh or Frozen chicken? Well, I have tried both and in my opinion fresh is better but more expensive, however Adey showed me a neat trick which if using frozen chicken gets great results: simply rinse the chicken thoroughly in water for 10 minutes to remove the saline solution which they pump into frozen chicken and the result is a more tender and tasty chicken - I must admit I was impressed!

The way you do this is to take your chicken fillets or breasts and put them in a clean stainless steel sink or large plastic tub and first soak the already defrosted chicken in some tepid water for about an hour at least, then rinse of the water and wash the individual fillets in tepid water {this helps them release more of the salt water}, wash thoroughly until the water starts to look clear and the chicken looks a little more pink in colour.

Korma or Masala Dishes - that something extra!

Adey's Tip. Have you ever had a Korma or Tikka Masala dish that had that 'something extra'? It may well be Almond essence. Adey informed me that to get that "Marzipan like taste…" add just a drop or two of Almond essence.

INGREDIENTS & METHOD {in order of use} – KORMA SAUCE

1. Onions (¼ filled) {finely sliced in a 5 Litre Pan}
2. Raisen & Sultana Mix (2 Chef's spoons)
3. Garlic & Ginger Paste (½ Chef's spoon)
4. Vegetable Oil (½ Chef's spoon)
5. Butter Ghee (½ Chef's spoon)
6. Heat-up and ensure Onions are fully coated with the mix.
7. Water (as reqd) {Cover the onions and simmer covered until the Onions have completely disintegrated!}
8. Blend cooled mixture until very very smooth.
9. Now add (equal quantities) {by volume} of Castor Sugar, Almond Powder, Coconut Flour and Single Cream. {The actual quantities required are determined by the consistency of the mix – PlayDough?}

Chef's Note. The Korma Sauce can be frozen into 'single-portions' for future use.

Tasty Rice Dishes

Rice doesn't have much flavour of its own and in the BIR they have a few nifty little tricks to add flavour and texture and here they are.

> **11**
>
> <u>Adey's Tip</u>. Add some crispy deep fried onions {they buy these ready done; we use the KTC brand} in to a Biryani or any fried rice dish to add a lovely intense flavour - Yum!

Have you ever ordered Pillau rice and they have served you brown looking rice that has a slightly nutty taste; then you have probably had Cumin fried rice. The word 'Pillau' rice is an almost generic term for any other rice than plain boiled white rice. Here is how you make it:

> INGREDIENTS {in order of use} – CUMIN FRIED RICE {SERVES 4}
>
> 1. Vegetable Oil (1 TBSP)
> 2. Cumin Powder (1 TBSP)
> 3. Cumin Seed (1 tsp)
> 4. Basmati Rice (1 Mug)
> 5. Water (1½ Mugs)
> 6. Salt (Pinch)
> 7. Butter Ghee (1 tsp) [OPTIONAL]
> 8. Akhni Stock (2 tsp) [OPTIONAL]

METHOD – CUMIN FRIED RICE {SERVES 4}

1. Take the Cumin Powder and mix with a little Water to form a paste.
2. Add the Oil to a pan and heat until hot enough to cause two 'test' Cumin Seeds to 'sizzle & pop'. Take the Cumin Paste and Seeds and add both to heated oil in the pan and cook for around 20 seconds - until it turns light brown {be careful not to burn it as nothing taste worse than burnt Cumin Seeds!}.
3. Now add the Basmati rice and stir into the spice mixture until all the rice turns light brown and fry together on a low to moderate heat for about 3 minutes or until the rice grains lose that opaque look. Now add the Water, Salt and stir once and on with the lid.
4. Once the rice is simmering wait about 4 ~ 5 minutes and take a peep. If the rice has lots of little hole in the mixtures it's almost done. Taste a grain and if it's al dente but not raw then turn the heat off put the lid on tight {if it won't fit tight, use a tea towel to make the pan airtight} then leave to steam for 10 mins.
5. After 10 mins remove the lid and separate with a fork. You should now have delicious Cumin Rice!

Another nifty trick in the BIR kitchen is to put a tsp of Butter Ghee in some hot rice just prior to serving. This adds that lovely glossy finish to the rice which so characterises BIR Pillau rice. Also, some Chefs add a tsp of Akhni stock {explained later in the chapter} to 1 ~ 2 portions of rice just prior to serving.

Adey Tip for Sour Dishes. If you are making a sour dish like say Pathia and you add in a little too much lemon, try adding a squeeze of fresh orange juice this helps balance the flavours and remove some of the sourness.

The Seasoned Oil Controversy!

Nothing I can think of has caused as much controversy and questioning as the subject of seasoned oil. You would not believe the amount of emails I get asking, "do you really need to add used vegetable oil to get that BIR taste"?

Many people are put off by the idea of putting in used oil into a dish. This is something that is done in many BIR kitchens and I have come to the conclusion that if you want to achieve restaurant like results then you have to do what they do in the restaurants. Having said all that, I do know of many BIR Chefs that don't use seasoned oil but infuse flavour into their curries in other ways. I mention one below.

Adey's Seasoned Oil Short-Cut

Adey has a quick method of making seasoned oil that is great if you don't fancy making 20 ~ 30 Onion Bhajis. Here it is:

INGREDIENTS – ADEY'S SEASONED OIL SHORT-CUT

1. Vegetable Oil (300ml)
2. Onions (4) {Diced Red or White}
3. Paunch Phoran (1 tsp)
4. Fennel Seeds (½ tsp)
5. Cumin Seeds (1 tsp)
6. Bay Leaves (2)
7. Garlic & Ginger Paste (1 TBSP)
8. Turmeric (½ tsp)

METHOD – ADEY'S SEASONED OIL SHORT-CUT

1. Add the onions and the whole spices into the hot oil and fry first for 1-3 minutes, make sure the oil is not too hot or you onions and spices will turn dark brown very quickly and the desired effect will be lost.
2. Just as the onions start to turn golden brown add in the Garlic
3. & Ginger Paste and the Turmeric and fry these for just a minute more.
4. Allow to cool and strain-off the whole ingredients - ***Done!***

Spiced Water {aka Akhni Stock}

INGREDIENTS & METHOD – SPICED WATER

1. Water (1.5 Ltrs)
2. Cumin Seeds (3 TBSP) {Brown}
3. Green Cardamoms (~15)
4. Black Cardamoms (3 ~ 4)
5. Cinnamon Sticks (4 ~ 5)
6. Cloves (3)
7. Star Anise (1)
8. Bay Leaves (few!) {Asian}

Add all the ingredients to the water and bring to the boil and then simmer on a medium heat for 30 minutes. Strain off the spices and retain for <u>one more</u> use!

A Chef's spoon (2 TBSP) of Spiced Water to any curry you wish. Some chefs add some of the whole spices that are generally strained off to certain dishes.

Lentil Based Dishes

It doesn't matter if you are a vegetarian or not, everyone loves Tarkha Dhal! I am surprised by how many people still do not realise how easy lentil based dishes are to cook and therefore avoid cooking them.

Traditionally Tarkha Dhal is made using red lentils which require no soaking and cook super quick. Channa and Mung dhal do require soaking for a few hours and can take a while to cook but if you own a pressure cooker *{I really recommend investing in one if you haven't already}* then you can cook these dhals in no time at all, in fact I have included a few of my favourite Dhal recipes in this book for you to try out.

Another objection to dhal based curries is the fact that some lentils and legumes can be a bit bitter to taste. I have included one of Adey's tips which works a treat - that is to add ½ tsp {for 2 ~ 4 portions} of Demerara sugar during the final cooking stage as this really balances out the dish well and helps remove any bitter element.

Since I have always preferred a more vegetarian style diet, and just recently in the last year gone back to a vegetarian diet, I eat a lot of Dhal based curries and I wish more people would try them not just for the wonderful taste and texture but also for their health benefits. Here are just a few to consider:

1. <u>Lower Cholesterol</u>. Lentils help to reduce blood cholesterol since they contains high levels of soluble fibre. Lowering your cholesterol levels helps reduce your risk of heart disease and stroke. This is achieved by keeping your arteries clean and interestingly scientists in Canada ran tests on patients who suffered from PAD {Peripheral Artery Disease} and found that when they consumed 4-6 portions of lentils, peas or legumes a week their arteries showed signs of a reversal of the disease. Do you think that is a good reason to eat them?

2. <u>Heart Health</u>. Many studies have now shown that eating high fibre foods like lentils and legumes dramatically reduces your risk of heart disease. Lentils and legumes are also a great source of folate {folic acid}

and magnesium, which are big contributors to heart health. Folate lowers your homocysteine levels, a serious risk factor for heart disease. Magnesium helps improves blood flow, oxygen and nutrients throughout the body. Low levels of magnesium have been directly associated with heart disease, so eating lentils will keep your heart health and happy!

3. <u>Good Digestive Health</u>.   Insoluble dietary fibre found in lentils, legumes and peas helps prevent bowel problems like constipation and other digestive problems such as irritable bowel syndrome and diverticulosis. It is no surprise that these problems are rare in south Asian countries but rife in the western world where our diet is generally lower in these super foods!

4. <u>Stabilise Blood Sugar</u>.   These fibre rich foods helps stabilise blood sugar levels as they have a low glycaemic index. In other words prevent insulin spikes in the blood.

5. <u>Good Protein</u>.   One question I know irritates many a vegetarian is: 'Where do you get your protein from if you don't eat meat?' Lentils, nuts and legumes are one of the best sources of digestible protein that you can eat. In other words the protein that these foods provide is more bio available to the human body, so even if you are a meat eater you should eat lentils and legumes.

I bet you feel hungry for a good dhal now! I know this chapter is all about cooking tips and techniques but I couldn't resist a little plug for the dhal based curries which, let's face it, are the most popular type of curry {if you can call it that} in many places in India, Pakistan and Bangladesh. It will generally be what the staff are eating in the Indian restaurant or takeaway you visit.

<u>Marinating</u>

In 'PART 1' I only touched on Marinating. Marinating your meat, chicken or fish not only adds flavour but also helps to tenderise it. In my 2 videos for Chicken Tikka Masala you get some tips on Marinating. There is also a video I did on

YouTube about marinating with some great tips in it. I just want to mention one or two more things about marinating your food. If you are wanting your meat nice and tender then using a plain low fat natural yoghurt will do the trick. You may try adding Amchoor powder {dried mango} - this is also used as a meat tenderiser. Finally, if you are short of time and haven't 24 hours to play with try this tip:

Flatten the meat with the palm of your hand and rub-in the spices directly to the meat, then add the meat to a bowl and add some low fat natural Yoghurt and 1 tsp of Amchoor powder and 1 TBSP of Lime juice. Rub into the meat all the ingredients and place the meat and marinade into a plastic zip lock bag, make sure to push all the air out of the bag before sealing. Leave the meat and marinate on a plate in the kitchen NOT in the fridge. In 2 Hours you will have wonderfully marinated meat or fish!

People generally don't think of marinating vegetables but Adey adds some methi leaves to his onions and peppers which he say help add more flavour. Also try sprinkling a little Tandoori Masala Powder over those raw veggies to infuse some flavour.

In Conclusion

The reason why I decided right from the beginning of this project to include a chapter on 'Tips & Tricks . . . .' was to help many a curry cooking enthusiast plug a few holes in their knowledge. Many of the tips, techniques and insights Adey and I have shared in this chapter have taken us many years to acquire and often with much trial and error as well as the invaluable training we have received from some Curry cooking Masters. One last word of advice {well, five actually} - *practice, practice and more practice!*

Chapter 5

More Base Gravy 'Secrets' revealed!

After a year of personally cooking around 8,000 individual curries for our local customers - yes I took an inventory of how many individual curries we had served - very anal I know! Well, anyway after a year of cooking a lot of curries using certain methods, ingredients and techniques I decided to add a few variations and see if I could improve on some of my dishes.

The Onion Base Gravy

As mentioned in my first e-book I had at least two other Base Gravy recipes that I had used at 'Curry 2 Go'; The Bangladeshi style and the Indian Style, which as I have already mentioned in that book were merely "styles" not necessarily exact recipes. As I mentioned at the beginning of this book in 'Back on the Curry Trail…' there are no exact set of rules or any one recipe that can therefore be determined as 'authentic,' 'actual,' or 'exact'.

By using terms like 'Bangladeshi and Indian' I was merely referring to certain styles and ingredients which I had observed over the years used in BIR restaurants - those run by Indian Chefs and those run by Bengali Chefs and those were the differences I had observed.

As mentioned in my first e-book, the 'Indian' style base gravy seemed to lend itself well to the sweeter type of curries like Passanda, Korma and Chicken Tikka Masala, whereas the Bangladeshi 'style' Base Gravy lends itself more to the spicier variety of curries, particularly those that utilise '**Seasoned Oil**'.

Hence I decided after trialling both bases for a time that I would come up with a Base Gravy recipe of my own that was a compromise of the two bases - hence the 'Curry 2 Go' Base Gravy was created and that recipe is included in my first book. If you haven't yet got that e-book you can get it here: http://www.curry2go-online.com/my-ebook--the-secret-to-that-takeaway-curry-taste.html

The reason I am reiterating all of these is that during my tweaking of those two bases I had remembered learning some years before of a Base Gravy recipe that was made from just Onions, Vegetable Oil, Water, Turmeric, Ground Coriander and Ground Cumin and I had heard that it produced surprisingly good results. This Base, I had heard, was the "original" Base Gravy used in 'Indian Restaurants' before the influence of the European stock took hold.

I decided to have a go at making it, though I had to admit I had never seen this one done personally myself or even had any definitive recipe, so I utilised much of the same principles as with the other Base Gravy recipes but just included Onions, Water, Vegetable Oil {not seasoned} and some 'MIX' Powder from a basic recipe of equal parts {by volume} of Turmeric, Coriander, Cumin, Paprika and Rajah mild Madras Curry Powder.

The first curry I made using this Base was a chicken Korma. The story goes like this:

I had decided to have a go at making this Base after we had closed following a busy Saturday trade and just as this new Base was being finished lo and behold there was a knock on the metal shutters of our unit which fronts straight onto the main street in Chorley. I opened the shutters and was greeted by one of my regular Saturday customers, a lady who worked locally in the town and who every Saturday religiously ordered the same meal - a 'Meal Deal for 1' with a chicken

Korma. Looking a bit harassed as if she had had a tough day she apologised for keeping us from closing by asking;

"Could you possibly make me my usual...."?

"Erm....should I use some of our regular Base Gravy that we had left, or should I trial this new Base recipe?" I mused.

I couldn't resist experimenting with this loyal customer and the resulting Korma from this Onion Base was honestly one of the best chicken Kormas I had ever tasted - and I am not even a fan of chicken Korma!

I was that impressed with this Base Gravy that I ran with it for about three months with all our curries from then on. In time, however, I noticed one or two curries on the menu tasted slightly better with our regular base so eventually we devised the 'Curry 2 Go' Base Gravy. Hence I didn't include the recipe for this Onion Base Gravy in my first book but thought I would add it in my next. So here it is. The reason why I think this recipe makes for such a good Base is that it's made from the most flavourful ingredient of any of the Base Gravy ingredients - onions!

The 'Original' Onion Base Gravy
3 Litre version

 https://youtu.be/Hs6BEEhsVU4

INGREDIENTS 1 – 'ORIGINAL' ONION BASE GRAVY

1. Onions (3 litre pan filled 2 ~ 3cms from the top) {Dutch or English variety, peeled & quartered}
2. Water (300ml)
3. Vegetable Oil (150 ml) {not olive oil as it won't taste right!}

METHOD 1 – 'ORIGINAL' ONION BASE GRAVY

Put the pot of ingredients on the stove-top on a low heat. Don't be tempted to put the flame a bit higher to speed things along as your ingredients will burn. As always with BIR cooking - have patience!

Put the lid on. The pot should not be overflowing with ingredients as with other Base recipes, but it's important to put the lid on so that there is no loss of liquid yet!

It will take about 30 minutes before the ingredients come up to heat and you notice any bubbling. As I explained in my first e-book, and I am going to re-iterate here for those who may not have yet got that book, you must cook the onions for the correct length of time till completely soft and translucent.

 The knife test will help you determine if the onions are cooked enough - simply take a sharp knife and poke one of the onions. If it's cooked enough there should be no resistance at all.

Once your onions are cooked, we are now ready for the spices.

INGREDIENTS 2 – 'ORIGINAL' ONION BASE GRAVY

1. Vegetable Oil (1 TBSP)
2. Garlic & Ginger Paste (2 TBSP)
3. 'MIX' Powder (4 h/tsp)

METHOD 2 – 'ORIGINAL' ONION BASE GRAVY

1. Add vegetable Oil to a pan and heat.
2. Next add the Garlic & Ginger Paste and fry for 1 min or until the water has evaporated.
3. Then add the 'MIX' Powder and fry for 1 min to help release their flavours and add some water from the 'Onion Pot' to make a paste.
4. Add the 'paste' to the simmering onion mixture.

INGREDIENTS 3 – 'ORIGINAL' ONION BASE GRAVY

1. Salt (1½ tsp)
2. Water (350ml) {2 mugs}
3. Demerara Sugar (1 h/tsp) {Brown sugar adds a sweet element that really compliments the Base Gravy}

METHOD 3 – 'ORIGINAL' ONION BASE GRAVY

1. Add the Salt, Water and Sugar to the 'Onion Pot' and stir well.
2. Allow the mixture to continue for another 30 mins.
3. Remove from the heat and allow to cool.
4. Blend until completely smooth.
5. Add 2 Litres of water and blend for final consistency. Done!

My observations about this Onion Base Gravy. What I particularly like about this Base, is its simplicity both in making it and in its taste. At home when I make Base Gravy I make this Base, not only because it's easy to make, but also because it allows the Chef more control in bringing out different characteristics in the actual curry utilising perhaps more whole spices and it tends to create curries with less of a tainted taste than some other Base Gravies.

> Some Base Gravy recipes can be over seasoned and end up producing curries that all taste the same - some of you will know what I mean!
>
> This Onion Base demonstrates a certain truth - less is more!

Curried Away's Base Gravy

This recipe is one from Adey and is a great Base that produces some really tasty curries, like his famous Chicken Tikka Patia! {https://youtu.be/Ujw82lBg3Cg} You've got to try it! Thanks Adey!

{3 Litre Pan version}

INGREDIENTS 1 – CURRIED AWAY'S BASE GRAVY

1. Onions ($^9/_{10}$ panful) {English - peeled and quartered}
2. Red Pepper (¼) {capsicum}
3. Green Pepper (¼) {capsicum}
4. Carrot (½) {roughly chopped}
5. Potato (½) {Cubed - Low starch variety, e.g. Desiree or other red skinned type}
6. Coriander (½ a bunch) {Fresh - roughly chopped}
7. Ginger Root (5cm piece) {With skin - roughly chopped}
8. Tomatoes (2-3 medium) {Fresh – quartered}
9. Garlic & Ginger Paste (5 TBSP)
10. Tomatoes (400g tin) {Plum}
11. Cabbage (¼) {White – small - coarsely chopped}
12. Green Chillies (2) {with seeds}
13. Turmeric (1½ TBSP)
14. Vegetable Oil (300 ml)
15. Water (500 ml)
16. Salt (1 TBSP)

METHOD 1 - CURRIED AWAY'S BASE GRAVY

Put all these ingredients on the stove - lid on - and bring to a boil.

Once boiling, adjust the heat for a medium to vigorous simmer.

For the spices you will need for this recipe:

INGREDIENTS 2 - CURRIED AWAY'S BASE GRAVY

1. Bay Leaves (4)
2. Cinnamon Stick (5cm piece)
3. Cardamoms (2-3)
4. Cumin Powder (½ tsp)
5. 'MIX' Powder (1 h/tsp)

METHOD 2 - CURRIED AWAY'S BASE GRAVY

Take a frying pan and add 4 TBSP of veg oil, leave on the heat until the oil is hot {important!}. Add the bay leaves, they should crackle not turn dark brown though {if they do the oil is too hot!}. Next add the rest of the whole spices and stir around the pan for about 30 seconds. Now add the 'MIX' Powder and Cumin Powder and stir for another 30 seconds then strain off any excess oil and add these cooked spices to the gravy pot.

METHOD 3 - CURRIED AWAY'S BASE GRAVY

Stir all the ingredients together and cook until the onions are soft and translucent and the oil has begun to rise to the top; once this happens take off the heat, leave to cool. Then remove the Bay Leaves, Cinnamon Stick and Cardamom Husks and blend until completely smooth.

Note: Adey has his Gravy mixture quite thick and adds water as and when required depending on the dish he's making, however he says there is no problem adding water to this finished gravy to get the desired consistency you prefer.

Pakistani Style Base Gravy

If you have read the chapter 'The Mancunian Way' you will be aware that my early influences came from the Pakistani version of BIR and I still to this day prefer it over the Bengali style though having said that I am generalising really as I have eaten in some superb Bengali run restaurants that are hard to beat and also eaten in some poor Pakistani run restaurants. While many of us who regularly eat in Curry Houses might not be able to tell whether the establishment is Pakistani or Bengali run, there are a few clues that will give it away.

Pakistani run establishments often don't serve alcohol due to their strict Muslim beliefs and while, yes, most Bengalis are Muslim too they seem to have a more liberal interpretation of the rules as it were. Also, Pakistani run Curry Houses tend to feature dishes like 'Handi' 'Lahori Chicken', 'Nihari', 'Karahi', 'Haleem' and 'Shahi' as well as the usual Korma, Madras, Balti and Bhuna.

Personally I find the Pakistani style of BIR often tastier; this is in part due to the use of meat stock in their curries as well as a more liberal use of whole spices as in authentic Indian cuisine. Many dishes also do not make use of Base Gravy, this type of Curry cooking creates a completely different taste altogether.

However, just as authentic Bengali food is very different from what is served in most Bengali run BIR establishments the same can be said of many Pakistani run BIR Curry Houses. I discovered that they, like their Bengali counterparts also utilize a Base Gravy particularly in the 'Traditional' British style curries: Bhuna, Balti, and Chicken Tikka Masala etc...

Their version is different and I am going to share a recipe that I observed being prepared by a Chef at the Karachi in Bradford. Here it is...

{3 Litre Pan version}

INGREDIENTS – PAKISTANI STYLE BASE GRAVY

1. Chicken Carcass (½) {Uncooked - they normally remove all the meat for other dishes}
2. Onions (to fill pan) {Peeled and roughly sliced}
3. Vegetable Oil (100 ml)
4. Carrots (2) {Chopped}
5. Green Chillies (4) {The Asian variety}
6. Black Cardamoms (2)
7. Green Cardamoms (4)
8. Coriander Powder (1 TBSP) {Freshly ground if possible}
9. Cumin Powder (1 TBSP) {Freshly ground if possible}
10. Methi Leaves (1 TBSP)
11. Asian Bay Leaves (2) {Tej Patta}
12. Cinnamon Stick (5cm piece)
13. Turmeric Powder (1 tsp)
14. Black Cloves (4)
15. Black Peppercorns (10)
16. Garlic (1 TBSP) {Minced}
17. Salt (1 tsp)
18. Red Chillies (2 Large) {Dried red chillies - Kashmiri style}

The Chef from the Karachi in Bradford explained to me that they always grind 2 spices fresh - coriander and cumin and do not buy these spices pre-ground because the difference in taste is markedly different.

I have noticed this practice before in more authentic style of Pakistani cooking and it's something I have yet to see in a Bengali style BIR. Freshly ground coriander seed is like a completely different type of spice from the commercially ground varieties - try it!

METHOD – PAKISTANI STYLE BASE GRAVY

Cover all those ingredients with water, leaving about an inch gap at the top of the pan and bring to a vigorous simmer.

Place the lid on the pan leaving a small gap for the steam to escape and Boil the ingredients together for about an hour.

Allow the liquid to cool, and then remove the carcass from the pot ensuring there is no bone or gristle left in the pot.

Next, remove the husks from the black and green cardamoms making sure to squeeze out those aromatic seeds, remove also the stick cinnamon and bay leaves.

Blend the rest of the ingredients together until you have thick but smooth gravy. This gravy will form a jelly like consistency when cold and you can add a little water when cooking to achieve the desired consistency.

You will be amazed how good the curries taste that you make from using this Gravy! They use this Gravy in both Lamb and Vegetables dishes, though not suitable for Vegetarians.

Just a note about Pakistani curries as compared to Bengali curries. Pakistani curries generally have a thicker sauce and less of it, so bare this in mind when making curries using this base. As mentioned above you can add a little water with this thicker style gravy if you prefer a thinner consistency, but you may lose some of that lovely stock induced flavour that the chicken bones lend to this base. Enjoy!

Chapter 6

More Restaurant & Takeaway Style Curries

'The Secret of That Takeaway Curry Taste – Part 1' included what is generally considered the 'Traditional' Restaurant Style curries - Bhuna, Balti, Jhalfrezi etc...

In Part 2 my aim was to not only include more 'Traditional' BIR curry recipes but also some 'House Specialities' as well as some staff curries and Pakistani curry recipes.

In this chapter we will focus on some more BIR style curries and some 'House Specialities' too.

When I first visited Adey and his team in Lincolnshire and sampled some of his curries I knew I had to get some of his recipes in this book too!

As I have already mentioned many curry recipes are the invention of a particular restaurant or Chef, whereas the so called 'traditional' ones generally follow the same recipe with some twists and variations.

I have included such a variation in this chapter, a Chicken Madras, the recipe I got from an Indian Restaurant owner in Fuerteventura of all places! I have called this recipe 'Epic' Madras; look out for this one as I know you are going to love it!

So are you ready for 'Curry Curry Curry'!

Chicken Chasni

 https://youtu.be/Z2oluibfsr0

One of the least known BIR curries; rumour has it that this Curry has its origins in Glasgow {I can well believe that!} and apparently it was created in an effort to offer an 'Indian' version of the popular Chinese 'Sweet & Sour' dish. Whether that is true or not I am not sure but this dish, like its Chinese counterpart, incorporates Heinz tomato ketchup. It is surprisingly tasty!

INGREDIENTS {in order of use} – CHICKEN CHASNI

1. **Seasoned Oil** (1 Chef's spoon)
2. Garlic & Ginger Paste (1 tsp)
3. Methi Leaves (1 tsp)
4. Tomato Paste (1 Chef's spoon)
5. 'MIX' Powder (1 TBSP)
6. Chilli Powder (1 tsp)
7. Tandoori Masala (¼ tsp) {TAD}
8. Chicken (6~8 pieces) {pre-cooked}
9. Base Gravy (⅓ Ladle) {to loosen mix}
10. Onions (1 H/Chef's spoon) {Diced}
11. Base Gravy (⅓ Ladle) {to loosen mix}
12. Heinz Tomato Ketchup (½ Chef's spoon)
13. Tomato (1) {Medium, finely diced}
14. Base Gravy (⅓ Ladle) {to loosen mix}
15. Tamarind Sauce (½ Chef's spoon)
16. Mango Chutney (1 h/tsp) {include some solids}
17. Demerara Sugar (1 tsp)
18. Salt (Good Pinch) {DASH}
19. Base Gravy (1 Ladle)
20. Masala Sauce (1 TBSP) {aka Magic sauce}
21. Coriander to Garnish

METHOD – CHICKEN CHASNI

1. Heat up the oil in the pan.
2. Add the Garlic & Ginger Paste and Methi Leaves and cook until the water evaporates from the Garlic & Ginger Paste.
3. Add in the Tomato Paste and spices: 'MIX' Powder, Chilli Powder and Tandoori Masala and combine together and cook for 30 seconds.
4. Next, in with the pre-cooked chicken and coat in the spice mixture.
5. Add in about a third a ladle of Base Gravy to loosen the mixture.
6. Now, add in the chopped onions and cook in the sauce by turning up the heat slightly. As the sauce thickens add a little bit more Base Gravy.
7. Next, add the Heinz Tomato Ketchup and the diced Tomato.
8. Keep adding a little more Base Gravy as the sauce thickens.
9. Add the Tamarind Sauce.
10. Reduce the heat now and add the Mango Chutney.
11. Next add in the Sugar and Salt.
12. Now at this stage add a ladle of Base Gravy, cook for a minute then reduce the heat and simmer.
13. Once the oil floats to the top of the curry add in the Tikka Masala Sauce.
14. Cook for another minute then Garnish with some coriander leaves and finely sliced Spring Onions. **Done**!

Chef's Note. It's also nice to garnish with finely sliced Spring Onions. We ran out on the day of filming – *Doh!*

Lamb Passanda

 https://youtu.be/NyOJd4ohB3c

"The Favourite one..." Apparently that is what the Urdu word "pasande" means. So named because it was the choice of the Moghul Emperors of India. The original Indian dish was made with Lamb, hence this recipe is for a Lamb Passanda.

INGREDIENTS {in order of use} – LAMB PASSANDA

1. Seasoned Oil (1 Chef's spoon)
2. Onion (1 H/Chef's spoon) {Finely chopped onions softened *not* browned, try adding a little water to prevent browning}
3. Garlic & Ginger Paste (1 tsp)
4. Tomato Paste (1 Chef's spoon)
5. 'MIX' Powder (1 TBSP)
6. Salt (¼ tsp) {TAD}
7. Base Gravy (½ Ladle)
8. Lamb (6~8 Pieces) {Pre-cooked}
9. Base Gravy (½ Ladle)
10. Almond Powder (1 Chef's spoon) {Skant}
11. Yoghurt (1½ Chef's spoons) {Low fat natural}
12. Sugar (1 tsp) {Brown}
13. Mango Chutney (1 tsp)
14. Base Gravy (1 Ladle)
15. Single Cream (~ 2 Chef's spoons)
16. Garnish with a swirl of single cream and toasted Almonds flakes

METHOD – LAMB PASSANDA

1. Heat the oil in the pan. Once hot add in the onions and sauté - do *NOT* brown - just add a little water to prevent browning.
2. Add Garlic & Ginger Paste.
3. Next, add in the Tomato Paste and cook for a minute.
4. Add in the 'MIX' Powder.
5. Then add in the salt.
6. Now add in about a ½ ladle of Base Gravy to loosen the mixture.
7. Add in the Lamb.
8. As the mixture thickens add a little bit more Base Gravy.
9. Next add in the Almond powder. Once dissolved add in the yoghurt.
10. Turn down the heat and add in the sugar and the Mango Chutney.
11. Simmer together until the oil floats on the top then add in the 2nd ladle of Base Gravy, then simmer the mixture for about 2 minutes.
12. Next add in the single cream, stir in and add in the toasted almond flakes.
13. Serve up! ***Done!***

Chef's Note. Swirl on a little Single Cream and toasted Almond Flakes for appearance.

Chicken Sambar

 https://youtu.be/Zi9QYoRNJVg

Do you remember how I told you that sometimes the addition or omission of just one ingredient can create a completely new dish?

Well, this dish is a perfect example of that. This recipe utilises red lentils but feel free to try other lentils or beans like mung.

INGREDIENTS {in order of use} – CHICKEN SAMBAR

1. Seasoned Oil (1 Chef's spoon)
2. Garlic & Ginger Paste (1 tsp)
3. Methi Leaves (1 tsp)
4. Tomato Paste (1 Chef's spoon)
5. 'MIX' Powder (1 TBSP)
6. Chilli Powder (1 tsp)
7. Chicken (6~8 pieces) {pre-cooked}
8. Base Gravy (½ Ladle)
9. Patia Sauce (1 Chef's spoon)
   {click here: http://www.curry2go-online.com/recipes.html}
10. Base Gravy (1 Ladle)
11. Lentils (2 Chef's spoons) {pre-cooked - we use a mix of red and toor dhal}
12. Salt (¼ tsp) {TAD}
13. Tikka Masala Sauce (1 tsp)
14. Tandoori Masala (1 generous pinch) {DASH}
15. Garnish with fresh coriander. ***Done!***

METHOD – CHICKEN SAMBAR

1. Heat the oil in the pan.
2. Once the oil is hot, add the Garlic & Ginger Paste.
3. Next, add the Methi Leaves and cook for a minute.
4. Add the Tomato Paste and cook out for 30 seconds.
5. Now add the 'MIX' Powder and Chilli Powder and cook the spices for 30 seconds to a minute.
6. Add the pre-cooked chicken and coat in the spice mixture.
7. Now add a little Base Gravy about ½ a ladle.
8. Once you notice the oil floating on the top, it's time to add a little bit more Base Gravy.
9. Next, add in the Pathia sauce and stir in well.
10. Once the sauce has thickened and the oil has separated add the other ladle of base gravy.
11. Then add in the pre-cooked lentils and the salt.
12. Now add in the tsp of Tikka Masala Sauce and cook further for 2 minutes.
13. After that, add in a good pinch of Tandoori Masala and a sprinkle of fresh coriander leaves. ***Done!***

<u>Chef's Note</u>. If you want more texture in the sauce use mung dhal instead.

Lamb Tikka Balti Roshan

"What is a Balti Roshan?" I here you ask. Well the short explanation is a Balti with attitude. Basically this is a Balti curry but with fresh chillies incorporated into the dish to create that sharp heat that Jalfrezi is known for but with the sumptuous texture and taste of a Balti dish - in my opinion a fantastic fusion! Here is how you make it:

INGREDIENTS – LAMB TIKKA BALTI ROSHAN

1. **Seasoned Oil** (1 Chef's spoon)
2. Onions (1½ Chef's spoons) {finely diced}
3. Patak's Balti Paste (1 TBSP)
4. Garlic & Ginger Paste (1 tsp) {generous}
5. Tomato Paste (½ Chef's spoon)
6. Methi Leaves (1 tsp)
7. Chilli Powder (½ tsp)
8. 'MIX' Powder (1 TBSP) {scant}
9. Lamb Tikka (6~8 pieces) {pre-cooked}
10. Base Gravy (2 Ladles)
11. Chillies (4) {medium}
12. Peppers & Onions (2 Chef's spoons) {pre-fried 'Shashlick Style'}
13. Salt (¼ tsp) {TAD}
14. Onions (1 H/Chef's spoon) {deep fried onions - shop bought variety}
15. Coriander to garnish

METHOD – LAMB TIKKA BALTI ROSHAN

1. Heat the oil in the pan.
2. Once hot add in the diced onions and sauté (add a little water).
3. Add in the Patak's Balti Paste and Garlic & Ginger Paste and fry together.
4. Next, add in the Tomato Paste.
5. Now add in the Methi, Chilli and 'MIX' Powder and fry off the spices.
6. Add in the Lamb and some of the stock.
7. Then add a little Base Gravy and the chillies.
8. After that toss in the pre-fried peppers and onions and incorporate into the dish.
9. Put in the Salt and keep the dish dry and moving around the pan.
10. Afterwards add in the other ladle of Base Gravy.
11. Cook further for 2 minutes. Once the sauce has thickened and the oil floats on the top add the pre-fried onions.
12. Serve and Garnish with coriander. ***Yum!***

<u>Chef's Note</u>. 'Shashlick Style' is a method cooking large slices of Red & Green Peppers and Onions by deep frying them in hot oil {160°C} for about 1 minute, this keeps the integrity of the peppers and onions whilst removing the raw taste.

Utilise pre-fried onions to add a lip smacking yumminess to any curry dish!

Lamb Tikka Tamarina

 https://youtu.be/RZcOg4zQYdg

This dish incorporates a true 'Indian' taste - that of Tamarind. In India the fruit of the Tamarind tree is used to sour certain dishes like Vindaloo and this one. In the BIR kitchen a Tamarind condiment is often used instead. A good variety I use is the 'Maggi' Tamarind sauce. This curry will be a delight for all those who like the sweet & sour taste but with some spice! The dish works best with Lamb but you can make it with chicken, fish or vegetables.

INGREDIENTS {in order of use} – LAMB TIKKA TAMARINA

1. **Seasoned Oil** (1 TBSP)
2. Onion (2 TBSP) {Finely diced}
3. Kashmiri Masala Paste (1 tsp) {Patak's}
4. Garlic & Ginger Paste (1 tsp)
5. Tomato Paste (2 TBSP)
6. 'MIX' Powder (½ TBSP)
7. Chilli Powder (¼ tsp)
8. Tandoori Masala Powder (¼ tsp) {Tad}
9. Salt (Pinch) {Small, to help soften the onions}
10. Lamb (8 bite-size pieces) {Pre-cooked Lamb Tikka}
11. Lamb Stock (2 TBSP)
12. Base Gravy (150 ml) {1st Ladle}
13. Mr Naga Pickle (⅓ tsp)
14. Tamarind Sauce (1½ TBSP)
15. Base Gravy (150 ml) {2nd Ladle}
16. Salt to taste
17. Shallots (2 TBSP) {Sliced}
18. Fresh coriander and a swirl of single cream to garnish.

METHOD – LAMB TIKKA TAMARINA

1. Warm your oil in the pan. Once warmed add the finely diced onions and fry on a moderate heat.
2. After about a minute just as the onions soften slightly add the Kashmiri Masala Paste and fry for another minute.
3. Now add in the Garlic & Ginger Paste and fry off till aromatic.
4. Next add in the Tomato Paste and fry for 30 seconds.
5. Now add in the 'MIX' Powder and cook in for about 30 seconds.
6. Next add in the Chilli Powder and the Tandoori Masala Powder.
7. Add in a small pinch of salt at this stage as it helps soften the onions.
8. Next add in the pre-cooked Lamb and the stock, coat in the spice mixture.
9. Now add the 1st ladle of base gravy to loosen the mix.
10. Next, add the Naga pickle.
11. Now add in the Tamarind sauce and cook on a high flame for about a minute to cook-out the tartness from the vinegar.
12. Next add the 2nd ladle of base gravy and cook on a 'low-light'.
13. Once the sauce has thickened and the oil has risen to the surface add some more salt to taste and stir in the spring onions.
14. Garnish with a swirl of fresh single cream and plenty of fresh coriander.

'Epic' Madras

 https://youtu.be/xak-SjaB8vk

This recipe was inspired by the 'Royal Tandoori Restaurant' in Corralejo Fuerteventura, which sadly is no longer there but has been replaced with a Tapas bar. The owner of this restaurant kindly gave me this recipe as I regularly ordered it from there after we moved from Lanzarote to Fuerteventura in 2005. I have tweaked his recipe and come up with what I can only describe as 'Epic'. This recipe is a chicken one but feel free to add meat, fish or vegetables. The thing that made this Madras 'Epic' are the green chillies. The owner of the Royal Tandoori used to specially import his green chillies from Gran Canaria, in order to achieve a particular taste, a fact he would often boast about.

INGREDIENTS {in order of use} – 'EPIC' MADRAS

1. **Seasoned Oil** (1 Chef's spoon)
2. Onions (1 Chef's spoon) {very finely diced}
3. Methi Leaves (1 tsp)
4. Green Pepper (½) { *very* finely chopped}
5. Green Chillies (3) {finely chopped with seeds – add at same time as Green Peppers – not shown in video!}
6. Garlic & Ginger Paste (1 tsp)
7. Tomatoes (2) { *very* ripe and *very* finely diced}
8. Turmeric (½ tsp)
9. Coriander Powder (1 h/tsp)
10. Cumin Powder (1 tsp)
11. Chicken (6~8 pieces) {pre-cooked}
12. Salt (½ tsp)
13. Patak's Chilli Pickle (½ tsp)
14. Base Gravy (1 Ladle) {1st Ladle}

15. Coriander Stalks (1 TBSP) {very finely chopped}
16. Coriander Leaves (1 TBSP)
17. Lime (¼ wedge) {Lemon used in video!}
18. Coconut Flour (½ tsp)
19. Base Gravy (1 Ladle) {2nd Ladle}
20. Garam Masala (sprinkle)

METHOD – 'EPIC' MADRAS

1. Heat the oil in the pan.
2. Fry the Onions on a fairly high heat for about 1 minute.
3. Put the Methi Leaves and cook for 30 seconds.
4. Add in the Green Capsicum and the Chillies and fry together for about a minute.
5. Now, add the Garlic & Ginger Paste and cook for 30 seconds.
6. Put in the Tomatoes and their juice and cook for 1 minute.
7. Add in the spices: Turmeric, Cumin and Coriander Powder and turn up the heat slightly to cook out the spices until you can smell them.
8. Then add the pre-cooked Chicken.
9. Add in the Salt.
10. Next, add in the Chilli Pickle and cook for 1 minute.
11. Now add in 1 ladle of the Base Gravy and stir in, cook on a high flame.
12. Once the oil rises in the pan, add in the second ladle of Base Gravy and continue to cook on a high flame.
13. Once the oil rises to the surface add in the Coriander Stalks, Garam Masala, and Coconut Flour and cook for a further minute.
14. Lower the heat and when the oil has again risen to the surface then add the Coriander Leaves and squeeze the juice from the wedge of Lime. ***Done!***

Chef's Note. The use of green chillies instead of chilli powder makes for a much tastier curry and is called in the Asian community 'Apni' style or Asian style. Also, when you cook spices in a lot of liquid like this dish always crank up the heat!

Lamb Naath
{Naat Yakkhn – Yogurt Lamb}

 https://youtu.be/2_kHqUeRl7o

This deliciously rich and tasty lamb dish has its origins in Kashmir India and utilises aromatic and pungent spices. The dish is not usually seen on many BIR menus but more and more British Indian restaurants are adding this tasty curry to the 'Speciality' section of their menus. If you like Lamb curries with a rich tasty, but not particularly hot and spicy sauce, then this is the dish for you!

INGREDIENTS {in order of use} – LAMB NAATH

1. **Seasoned Oil** (1 Chef's spoon)
2. **Green Pepper** (1 TBSP) { *very* finely diced}
3. Onions (1 Chef's spoon) { *very* finely diced}
4. Methi Leaves (1 tsp)
5. Garlic Paste (1 tsp)
6. Patak's Kashmiri Masala Paste (1 tsp)
7. Tomatoes (2 Chef's spoons) {fresh, finely chopped}
8. Salt (½ tsp)
9. 'MIX' Powder (1 TBSP)
10. Base Gravy (½ Ladle) {1st half-ladle}
11. Lamb (6~8 pieces) {pre-cooked with a Chef's spoon of the stock}
12. Cloves (2) {count them in}
13. Base Gravy (½ Ladle) {2nd half-ladle}
14. Dark Soy Sauce (½ tsp)
15. Base Gravy (½ Ladle) {3rd half-ladle}
16. Cloves (-2) {count them out}
17. Mango Chutney (1 tsp)

18. Yoghurt (2 TBSP) {plain low fat}
19. Garam Masala (sprinkle)
20. Coriander to garnish
21. Dribble of Yoghurt to Garnish.

METHOD – LAMB NAATH

1. Heat the pan on a medium heat and add the oil.
2. Once hot add in the Green Pepper and Onions and cook for 1 minute.
3. Next add in the Methi Leaves and Garlic Paste and cook out for 30 seconds.
4. Next add in the Kashmiri Masala Paste.
5. Now add in the chopped tomatoes and cook out for 1-2 minutes.
6. Next add in the Salt, 'MIX' Powder and cook out the spices for about a minute.
7. Now add the 1st half-ladle of Base Gravy and turn up the heat slightly.
8. Next add in the pre-cooked Lamb and some of the stock.
9. Add in the 2 Cloves.
10. Now add the 2nd half-ladle of Base Gravy.
11. Add in the Dark Soy Sauce and stir in well.
12. Next add in the 3rd half-ladle of Base Gravy and let the curry simmer until the sauce has thickened.
13. Remove both Cloves.
14. Next add in the Mango Chutney and stir in.
15. Reduce the heat and add the Yoghurt to the dish and once the oil rises to the surface add the Garam Masala.
16. Serve up and garnish with fresh Coriander and a dribble of Yoghurt.

Done!

Jhalfrani {Curried Away}

 https://youtu.be/GxzpDIwJKjw

Adey shared this curry recipe with us from 'Curried Away' and it tastes great! This sweet and delicious curry is for all those who love Masala style curries, Kormas and Passanda. I wasn't sure about this recipe when Adey described it to me as a curry he would like featured in the e-book, but I have to say it tastes great.

INGEDIENTS {in order of use} – JHALFRANI

1. Vegetable Oil (1 Chef's spoon)
2. Garlic (2 Cloves) {fresh, sliced}
3. Onion (½) {sliced}
4. Tomato Paste (1 Chef's spoon)
5. Methi Leaves (pinch)
6. 'MIX' Powder (1 TBSP)
7. Salt (¼ tsp) {Tad)
8. Chilli Powder (1 tsp)
9. Garam Masala (1 tsp)
10. Base Gravy (½ Ladle)
11. Korma Sauce (1½ Chef's spoons) {recipe in Chapter 6}
12. Base Gravy (½ Ladle)
13. Chicken Tikka (6~8 pieces) {pre-cooked}
14. Single Cream (2~3 TBSP)
15. Coriander (sprinkle) {fresh, chopped}
16. Green Chillies (2) {chopped – red & green chilli in video!}
17. Garam Masala (pinch)
18. Butter Ghee (1 tsp)
19. After serving garnish with Single Cream, Coriander and flaked Almonds.

METHOD – JHALFRANI

1. Heat the oil on a medium flame.
2. Next add in the sliced garlic and cook till just turning slightly brown.
3. Add the sliced onions and cook until translucent.
4. Now add in the Methi Leaves, 'MIX' Powder, Salt, Chilli Powder and Garam Masala and cook out these spices for about 1 minute.
5. Now add in the first half-ladle of Base Gravy.
6. Now add in the 'Korma Sauce' mix thoroughly in the pan and cook on a medium to high heat.
7. Once reduced slightly, add in the second half-ladle of Base Gravy and reduce the heat slightly and simmer for 2-3 minutes.
8. Next add in the Chicken Tikka and gently stir in.
9. Next add the Single Cream and stir-in.
10. Now add the Coriander, Chillies followed by a pinch of Garam Masala and some Butter Ghee.
11. Serve up and garnish with some Single Cream, Coriander and flaked Almonds. ***Done!***

Chicken Malayan {Curried Away}

You know how I mention earlier in the book about how the addition or omission of just one ingredient can create a completely different curry that tastes completely different? Well, this is the perfect example. This Curry is basically a Chicken Korma with Pineapple and pineapple syrup. Here's how it's done...

INGREDIENTS {in order of use} – CHICKEN MALAYAN

1. **Seasoned Oil** (1 TBSP)
2. Cinnamon Stick (1 Piece)
3. Cloves (2)
4. Base Gravy (300ml) {2-Ladles}
5. Coconut Flour (2 TBSP) {not desiccated – the finer the better!}
6. Almond Powder (1 TBSP) {again the finer the better}
7. Sultanas (6) {Green}
8. Chicken (6~8 pieces) {Pre-cooked}
9. Sugar (1 H/TBSP)
10. Single Cream (1 TBSP)
11. Pineapple (6~8 pieces) {tinned}
12. Pineapple Syrup (1~2 TBSP)
13. Garam Masala (Good Pinch) {Added at the end}
14. Almonds (as reqd) {toasted flakes} [OPTIONAL]

METHOD – CHICKEN MALAYAN

1. Heat (2 TBSP) of Seasoned Oil on a moderate flame.
2. Now add the Cinnamon and the Cloves to the Oil and stir for a minute.
3. Now add 2 Ladles (300ml) of Base Gravy and turn up the heat a little.
4. Now add the Coconut, Almond and Sultanas and stir-in to avoid lumps.
5. Once the mixture is simmering add the pre-cooked Chicken.
6. Now add the Sugar.
7. Once the mixture is smooth {after about 3 minutes} and the Coconut and Almonds have dissolved, remove the Cinnamon and Cloves.
8. Next add in the pineapple and the syrup.
9. Add the Cream and stir-in, followed by a good pinch of Garam Masala and then serve immediately. ***Done!***
10. Garnish with toasted Almonds. [OPTIONAL]

Chicken Kashmir {Curried Away}

Simply follow the recipe for Chicken Malayan, but instead of adding in the Pineapple pieces and Pineapple Syrup just add Lychee pieces and Lychee Syrup and Wallah, you now have Chicken Kashmir - how easy was that?

Man v Curry

This recipe is straight from the 'Curry 2 Go' menu in Chorley. I could tell you some interesting stories about this curry - which I am not sure I should include in this book for fear that someone complains. I will say nothing more... I came up with this recipe when we opened 'Curry 2 Go' as a gimmick really to create a talking point in Chorley - it certainly did that! My aim was to create a curry that was so ridiculously hot that few would be able to finish it. The result was surprising, not only did some finish it, it became a talking point on Facebook and Twitter and I ended up with people coming from Wigan and Blackburn {20 miles away} to try to eat it. The Curry ended up with its own following and I had regulars that ordered it.

I used to dread an order coming in for this curry because it would choke me and everyone else working in the kitchen to death! I ended up wearing a mask which looked bizarre to people walking by. Why the name 'Man versus Curry'? Yes you guessed right, it was adapted from the TV show 'Man versus Food' and the name said it all! I recommend only making {and eating} this curry if you seriously like *ludicrously* hot curry! The curry discontinued after I sold 'Curry 2 Go' as Ratchada wasn't keen on making it. {I don't blame her!} *By the way I never ate this curry; all I could manage was a taste.* OK, enough of the waffle, so here goes:

INGREDIENTS {in order of use} - MAN v CURRY

1. **Seasoned Oil** (1½ Chef's spoons)
2. Methi Leaves (1 tsp)
3. Garlic Cloves (8) {sliced}
4. Rocket Chillies (30) {chopped}
5. Scotch Bonnet Chillies (10) {with seeds - Oh yes!}
6. Tomato Paste (1 Chef's spoon)
7. 'MIX' Powder (1 TBSP)
8. Salt (½ tsp)
9. Black Pepper Corns (1 tsp) {crushed}
10. Base Gravy (1 Ladle) {1st Ladle}
11. Birds Eye Chillies (1 Chef's spoon) {crushed}
12. White Chilli Powder (1 TBSP) {see Chef's notes under 'METHOD'}
13. Water (1 Chef's spoon)
14. Base Gravy (1 Ladle) {2nd Ladle}
15. Chicken (6~8 pieces) {or Lamb or Vegetables}
16. Mr Naga Pickle (1 TBSP)
17. Coriander Stalks (1 TBSP) {finely chopped}
18. Garam Masala (sprinkle) {to finish}
19. Garnish with fresh Coriander
20. Root Ginger (1 TBSP) {julienned}

Are you sure you want to make this??

METHOD – MAN v CURRY

1. Heat the seasoned oil in the pan.
2. Once fairly hot add in the Methi Leaves.
3. Then add in the garlic and fry just till it starts to change colour.
4. Now in with the rocket chillies {I recommend wearing a mask or you will choke}
5. After about a minute add in the Scotch Bonnet chillies and fry for 1-2 minutes.
6. Next in with the Tomato Paste and cook out for 30 seconds.
7. Now, add in the 'MIX' Powder, Salt and Peppercorns.
8. Add the first ladle of Base Gravy and turn up the heat.
9. Once the curry is bubbling away add in the crushed Birds Eye chillies - the curry will start to change to a more sinister colour!
10. Next add in the White Chilli Powder {**WARNING** do not breath in any of this}
11. Thoroughly mix into the sauce and cook for 1-2 minutes then take off the heat.
12. Now, I recommend you allow this to cool before the next step but on a busy Saturday we obviously never did.
13. Blend this hellfire curry sauce into a smooth paste.
14. Once thoroughly blended add it back to the pan, add a little water {1 Chef's spoon}, and the second ladle of Base Gravy.
15. Next in with your meat or vegetables of choice and bring to a simmer.
16. Now add in the Mr Naga Pickle.
17. Once the oil starts to separate add in the coriander stalks, Garam Masala.
18. Serve with the julienned ginger sprinkled on top with some fresh coriander leaves. ***Done!***

Chef's Note. White Chilli Powder tastes completely different from its red counterpart, I recommend the Hampshire foods variety or the Top Op brand on the 'Spices of India' website. Don't mistake this with white pepper!

Now for the Pakistani taste...

If you have had a glance at the chapter in this book - 'The Mancunian Way' - you will have already noticed my biased leaning towards Pakistani curries and cooking. I make no apology for that because, not only did this version of British Indian curry influence my own curry journey from the start, but I find that the sheer simplicity of their cooking style and the way they combine simple ingredients lends itself to some of the tastiest food I have ever had!

I will cover just a few recipes on this section of the book - one or two are more BIR style whereas the first one I will cover is the real deal in terms of the sort of curry Pakistani people eat or that you might find in Lahore.

How do you know if when visiting an 'Indian' Restaurant whether it is Pakistani, Bengali or Indian? Well there are a few clues to look out for, some of them I mention in the chapter - 'The Mancunian Way', but generally Pakistani's are Muslim as are most Bengali's, however the Pakistani Muslims are more strict and often you will find their restaurants don't serve alcohol also Bengalis are generally darker skinned. Dishes on the menu will give it away too.

The type of Pakistani restaurants I like to visit serve up a more typical menu rather than a BIR one, those are the dishes that in my opinion taste the best. This first recipe is one such example, see what you think...

Pakistani Lamb Karahi

This dish is inspired by the tastiest Lamb curry I have ever eaten at Kabana's in Manchester. This dish is an authentic Pakistani Lamb on the bone curry and not BIR style. If you like lamb curries I know you will absolutely love this curry.

It requires a pressure cooker to make and if you haven't yet got a pressure cooker I would really urge you to buy one because they come in so handy and there really isn't an alternative way of making this curry. This is traditionally a Mutton curry but Lamb is equally as good, the only difference being that Mutton has a slightly stronger flavour. If you have access to a good Asian butcher you may be able to get Mutton - ask for 'Nalli' which means bone with marrow for best flavour.

INGREDIENTS {in order of use} – PAKISTANI LAMB KARAHI

1. Lamb (1kg) {Lamb or mutton on the bone}
2. Water (1 mug)
3. Red Onion (4) {finely sliced}
4. Tomatoes (4~6) {ripe tomatoes}
5. Garlic & Ginger Paste (1 TBSP)
6. Asian Chillies (3~4) {with seeds and chopped}
7. Turmeric (1 tsp)
8. Coriander (1 TBSP) {often freshly ground by Pakistani Chefs}
9. Cumin (1 TBSP) {often freshly ground by Pakistani Chefs}
10. Chilli Powder (1 tsp) {good quality chilli powder}
11. Salt (1 tsp)
12. Vegetable Oil (3 Chef's spoons)
13. Root Ginger (1 TBSP) {julienned}
14. Yoghurt (2 TBSP) {plain low fat}
15. Coriander (2 good handfuls) {freshly chopped}

METHOD – PAKISTANI LAMB KARAHI

1. Add into the pressure cooker all the ingredients except the Oil, julienned ginger, Fresh coriander and yoghurt.
2. On with the lid and put on a high flame or heat.
3. Once the cooker reaches pressure let it cook on medium to high heat for about 25 minutes after which take off the heat and let cool for about 10 minutes till the pressure dissipates.
4. Meanwhile if you have a Wok or large pan put it on the stove and heat up the oil; once hot add in the oil the contents of the pressure cooker.
5. Cook this on a medium to high flame for about 10 minutes to thicken the sauce {there isn't much gravy with this dish but if it becomes too dry add a little water}.
6. Towards the end of the 8 minutes add in the yoghurt and mix in well.
7. Just before the end add in the fresh coriander and ginger. ***Done!***

Chicken Handi

 https://youtu.be/NGDe2UHzguQ

This delicious, very popular and traditional Pakistani dish has now found its way onto the BIR curry menu, particularly in Manchester and no doubt other places, so this recipe is for the BIR version as opposed to a traditional or authentic recipe. The thing that characterises this particular curry is the combination of flavours – spicy - slightly sweet - slightly sour. A rich tasty gravy with that typical Pakistani taste. The 'Handi' is the traditional Pakistani pot, clay or metal that the curry is cooked in, the pot has a lid and is cooked with the lid on, however you can use any pan with a lid to get the same effect.

INGREDIENTS {in order of use} – CHICKEN HANDI

1. Butter Ghee (1 Chef's spoon)
2. Onions (2 Chef's spoons) {finely diced}
3. Garlic & Ginger Paste (1 tsp)
4. Methi Leaves (1 tsp)
5. 'MIX' Powder (1 TBSP)
6. Green Chillies (2) {chopped}
7. Tomatoes (2 Chef's spoons) {finely diced ripe tomatoes}
8. Base Gravy (1 Ladle) {1st Ladle}
9. Chicken (6~8 pieces) {pre-cooked}
10. Salt (½ tsp)
11. Base Gravy (1 Ladle) {2nd Ladle}
12. Plain Yoghurt (2 Chef's spoons) {low fat}
13. Mango Chutney (1 TBSP)
14. Fresh coriander to garnish

METHOD – CHICKEN HANDI

1. Heat up the Ghee in the pan.
2. Next add in the finely diced onions on a medium heat and cover with a lid to allow the onions to sweat a little, about 3 minutes.
3. Next add in the Garlic & Ginger Paste.
4. Then add the Methi Leaves and 'MIX' Powder and cook-off the spices for about 1 minute.
5. Now add the Tomatoes and Chillies and cook out the tomatoes for about 1-2 minutes.
6. Now add in the first ladle of Base Gravy and mix well whilst turning-up the heat to high.
7. Now add in the pre-cooked chicken and the salt.
8. Once the sauce begins to thicken add the second ladle of Base Gravy.
9. After about 1-2 minutes turn down the heat and add the yoghurt, stir in well, then add in the mango chutney and cover the pan with a lid and cook for a further 3-4 minutes on a fairly low light.
10. After that remove the lid, the oil should have risen to the top, garnish with coriander and serve. ***Done!***

The next curry we are going to do is one that I have received a lot of requests for, 'Methi Murgh' or 'Methi Chicken.' However strangely we didn't get too many request for this dish at 'Curry 2 Go', it was hardly ever ordered. This is a very tasty dish and I particularly like the veggie counterpart of this dish - 'Aloo Methi', that dish is also covered in this book in the starters and sides chapter.

Before we get in to this particular dish, just a few words about fresh Fenugreek Leaves. Most curry enthusiasts are familiar with Kasoori Methi or dried Methi Leaves but not as familiar with the fresh variety. You can buy fresh Methi from most Indian and Asian grocers, you often see it in the section where the fresh Chillies, Coriander and Parsley are. They have a darkish green symmetrical leaf. They are used extensively in South Asian cooking and are reputed to offer profound health benefits.

Fresh Fenugreek has a bitter flavour and because of this many are put off using it. Here are some tips about using fresh Fenugreek:

1. Only use the leaves, do not use any part of the stem or your dish will be too bitter.
2. Wash the leaves thoroughly - I recommend about three times, but only just before you are about to use them.
3. When adding them to a dish, add the salt just after as this helps draw the liquid out from the Fenugreek and helps counteract that bitter taste.
4. You can freeze fenugreek fine, so don't worry about buying 2 or 3 bunches as they normally sell 2-3 bunches for less than £2.

OK, let's cook 'Methi Murgh' or Methi Chicken.

Methi Chicken

INGREDIENTS {in order of use} – METHI CHICKEN

1. Vegetable Oil (1 Chef's spoon)
2. Garlic & Ginger Paste (1 tsp)
3. Onions (1 H/Chef's spoon) {finely chopped}
4. Green Chilli (1) {finely chopped}
5. Tomatoes (2 Chef's spoons) {chopped}
6. 'MIX' Powder (1 TBSP)
7. Chilli Powder (½ tsp)
8. Chicken (6~8 pieces) {pre-cooked}
9. Base Gravy (1 Ladle) {1st Ladle}
10. Fenugreek Leaves (2 good handfuls) {fresh}
11. Salt (½ tsp)
12. Base Gravy (1 Ladle) {2nd Ladle}
13. Garam Masala (1 tsp)
14. Demerara Sugar (½ tsp)
15. Coriander (1 Chef's spoon) {fresh}

METHOD – METHI CHICKEN

1. Heat the oil up in the pan.
2. Next add in the Garlic & Ginger Paste and fry off for about a minute.
3. Now add in the Onions and Green Chilli and sauté for about a minute.
4. Next add in the tomatoes and turn up the heat to cook off the tomatoes for just about a minute.
5. Now, add in the 'MIX' Powder and Chilli Powder and cook those spices for about a minute.
6. Next add the pre-cooked Chicken and mix in and coat with spices.
7. Now, add the first ladle of Base Gravy and increase the heat.
8. Once the sauce is bubbling away, add in the Fenugreek Leaves, then salt - you need to cook this on a fairly high flame, stirring all the time to prevent it 'catching'.
9. Once the sauce has thickened add in the next ladle of Base Gravy.
10. Cook the sauce for another minute on a high flame then reduce the heat and simmer for about another 3 minutes - the Fenugreek Leaves should now have softened, if not cook till they appear soft.
11. Now add in the Garam Masala, Demerara Sugar and the fresh Coriander Leaves - stir in then serve. ***Done!***

Murgh Nawabi {Curried Away}
{aka Chicken Nuwabi}

 https://youtu.be/gbH4N_XBuWo

'Emperor's food' - this is one of those dishes from the Moghul period. Nawabi is the Arabic word for Emperor. They liked their dishes to be rich and tasty. You will often find this dish on the specials section of the BIR menu. There are many variations of this dish, some use Tandoor chicken as in this recipe from Abdul, however you can use chicken tikka pieces instead if you don't fancy chicken on the bone.

INGREDIENTS – MURGH NAWABI

1. **Seasoned Oil** (1 Chef's spoon)
2. Butter Ghee (½ Chef's spoon)
3. Garlic Cloves (3) {sliced sideways}
4. Garlic Paste (1 tsp)
5. Onion (1 TBSP) {chopped}
6. Keema Mince (1½ Chef's spoons) {see Part 1 Seekh kebab recipe}
7. Mr Naga Pickle (1 tsp)
8. Tandoori Chicken (2 pieces) {see Chef's note under 'METHOD'}
9. Tomato Paste (1 Chef's spoon)
10. Methi Leaves (1 tsp)
11. 'MIX' Powder (1 TBSP)
12. Salt (½ tsp)
13. Chilli Powder (½ tsp)
14. Garam Masala (½ tsp)
15. Base Gravy (2 Ladles)
16. Coriander (2 x sprinkles) {freshly chopped}
17. Tomato (¼) {fresh}
18. Butter Ghee (1 tsp) {for glossy finish}
19. Egg (1) {fried, yolk broken and a sprinkle of coriander}
20. Garnish with a few pieces of red and green pepper

METHOD – MURGH NAWABI

1. Heat up the Oil and Ghee in the pan.
2. Add in the sliced garlic and brown.
3. Next add 1 tsp of Garlic Paste and fry for ½ a minute.
4. Now add in the chopped onions.
5. Next add in the Keema Mince and fry together for 1 minute.
6. Add in 1 tsp of Mr Naga Pickle and mix in.
7. Now add in the 2 pieces of Tandoori Chicken.
8. Also add in the Tomato Paste and fry off.
9. Now add the Methi, 'Mix Powder', Salt, Chilli Powder and Garam Masala.
10. Now add in about ¾ Ladle of Base Gravy and mix in.
11. Sprinkle in some fresh coriander.
12. Next in with the next ladle (or just less) of Base Gravy.
13. Get the mixture to a nice simmer and add in ¼ tomato wedge.
14. As the dish is coming to a finish add in the Butter Ghee.
15. In a separate pan add in some oil and fry an egg - make sure to break the yolk and add a sprinkle of fresh coriander; we are looking for an omelette like consistency.
16. Serve the dish with the egg on top with one or two pieces of green and red pepper to garnish. ***Done!***

Chef's Note. To make chicken Tandoor style at home is easy. Simply marinate some chicken legs or wings in Tikka Masala Sauce and a squeeze of fresh lemon for 24 hours, then cook them on a baking tray covered with foil for about 20-25 minutes at 200 degrees, then remove the foil and place the tray at the top of the oven and cook for another 10 minutes. Check to make sure the chicken is cooked through before serving.

You can substitute Tandoor chicken on the bone for chicken tikka pieces.

Lamb Korahi {Curried Away}

 https://youtu.be/ol4TsnrD1FU

This is another one of those dishes that is named after the implement its cooked or served in. This is Adey's recipe and he raved on about it that much that we included it in the e-book. Here it is:

INGREDIENTS {in order of use} – LAMB KORAHI

1. **Seasoned Oil** (1 Chef's spoon) {or vegetable oil}
2. Butter Ghee (1 tsp)
3. Garlic (2 Cloves) {fresh, finely sliced}
4. Onion + Methi + Pepper Mix (H/Chef's spoon)
5. Tomato Paste (1 Chef's spoon)
6. Methi Leaves (1 Pinch)
7. 'MIX' Powder (1 TBSP)
8. Salt (touch)
9. Chilli Powder (< 1 tsp) {just under}
10. Garam Masala (touch)
11. Base Gravy (touch) {to loosen the mix} {Adey said Oil!}
12. Lamb (6~8 pieces) {pre-cooked – or your chosen veggies}
13. Base Gravy (1 Ladle) {1st Ladle}
14. Tomato (2 x ¼) {Fresh}
15. Lime (¼) {squeeze juice from - then add spent lime to the mix}
16. Coriander (handful) {fresh}
17. Spring Onion (1 Chef's spoon) {chopped}
18. Peppers (4 pieces ea) {Green & Red for colour and texture}
19. Base Gravy (1 Ladle) {2nd Ladle}
20. Coriander (a pinch) {fresh}
21. Butter Ghee (touch)

METHOD – LAMB KORAHI

1. Heat the oil in the pan with a medium flame.
2. Add the butter Ghee.
3. Add the sliced garlic and brown without burning.
4. Add in the chopped onions + peppers + methi mix and increase to a high flame.
5. Next add in the tomato paste.
6. Briskly fry the mixture and cook off the tomato paste.
7. Add a pinch of Methi and 1 TBSP of 'MIX' Powder.
8. Add the Salt, Chilli Powder, Garam Masala and a touch of base gravy to extend the cooking time of the spices. {add Base Gravy, as required, to keep the spices from burning}.
9. Add the pre-cooked lamb and cook in the spice mix before adding the first ladle of Base Gravy.
10. Add in 2 quarters of fresh tomato and a squeeze of lime juice.
11. Add a handful of fresh coriander and the spring onions.
12. Now add the green and red Peppers.
13. After the mix has reduced add the 2nd Ladle of Base Gravy.
14. Turn down the heat and simmer.
15. Next add in some fresh coriander and a touch of Butter Ghee.
16. Wait for the oil to float to the top and serve with some more fresh coriander. ***Done!***

Chef's Note. Add a ½ tsp of Mr Naga Pickle at the end of cooking for additional flavour.

Mixed Special Balti
{Curried Away}

 https://youtu.be/XkEqM1-kGWg

If you are one of those that says when visiting an 'Indian' Restaurant or takeaway - "I can't decide what to have, should I have Chicken or Lamb, or should I go for seafood for a change..." Then this speciality dish might be right up your street! Adey has very kindly shared one of Curried Away's speciality dishes with us, his 'Mixed Special Balti' Enjoy!

INGREDIENTS {in order of use} – MIXED SPECIAL BALTI

1. Butter Ghee (1 TBSP)
2. Garlic (4 cloves) {fresh, sliced}
3. Onions (1 Chef's spoon) {sliced}
4. Green & Red Peppers (handful) {roughly chopped chunks}
5. Methi Leaves (½ tsp)
6. 'MIX' Powder (½ TBSP)
7. Chilli Powder (½ tsp)
8. Tomato Paste (1 Chef's spoon)
9. Lemon (½) {Juice from}
10. Lamb & Chicken (4 pieces ea) {pre-cooked}
11. Prawns (handful) {fresh or pre-cooked}
12. Patak's Balti Paste (½ Chef's spoon)
13. Base Gravy (1 Ladle) {1st Ladle}
14. Salt (½ tsp)
15. Coriander (handful) {fresh}
16. Mr Naga Pickle (1 tsp)
17. Chaat Masala (½ tsp) {see Chef's notes under 'METHOD'}
18. Garam Masala (½ tsp)
19. Coriander to garnish

METHOD – MIXED SPECIAL BALTI

1. First, heat a pan on a medium flame and add the Butter Ghee.
2. When the Ghee has all melted add the garlic, onions, mixed peppers and Methi and cook together for about 30 seconds.
3. Now add the 'MIX' Powder, Chilli Powder and stir into the mixture briskly.
4. After about another 30 seconds add in the Tomato Paste and again stir into the mixture briskly and cook out for about 45 seconds.
5. Next add in the fresh lemon juice, Lamb, Chicken and Prawns.
6. Now add in the Balti paste and stir in briskly and cook for 30 seconds.
7. Next add in the first ladle of Base Gravy and stir in to the mixture.
8. Next add in the Salt, Coriander, Mr Naga Pickle, Chaat Masala, and Garam Masala, then cook together on a high heat for about 45 seconds.
9. Then reduce the heat and wait till the oil rises to the top, add some more fresh coriander to garnish. ***Done!***

Chef's Note. Chaat Masala (aka spelt chat) is a finishing spice, like Garam Masala it gives certain dishes that sweet and sour taste. The chaat masala is used in a lot of Indian and Pakistani street food and snacks.

This masala usually contains, black salt, anchoor (dried mango powder) cumin, hing, ginger and chilli powder. Be selective in your use of this masala and use it sparingly. It is great in vegetarian dishes and dhals and sprinkled on snacks like samosa.

Mr Naga

 https://youtu.be/hQjnGoRbaPc

This is my daughter's favourite curry and this recipe is thanks to the Chef at the Jononi Balti in Preston Lancashire. This dish is not a blindingly hot dish {as you might think} just because it's got Mr Naga Pickle in it. As many of you will have already discovered, Mr Naga Pickle is used mostly to add flavour not necessarily heat. This dish is a sweet and hot {Madras hot} dish with a luscious tomato sauce and one I recommend you cook, it's delicious!

I first went into the Takeaway that makes this curry about 2 years ago and as I was waiting for our order I could see all the kitchen staff talking together and looking over at me {It's an open plan kitchen} eventually the guy who took my order said, "Are you a TV Chef?" I said, "No" he said, "Our Chef recognises you..." I explained it must be from Youtube! They seemed honoured that I had come to their Takeaway and treated me like a bit of a celebrity. I have since returned and chatted with the owner and they are interested in me making some videos in their takeaway when I find the time – so keep your eye on my Youtube channel for other recipes from the 'Jononi Balti'.

INGREDIENTS {in order of use} – MR NAGA

1. Vegetable Oil (1 Chef's spoon)
2. Onions (1 Chef's spoon) {finely diced}
3. Methi Leaves (1 tsp)
4. Garlic & Ginger Paste (1 tsp)
5. Tomato Paste (1 Chef's spoon)
6. 'MIX' Powder (1 TBSP)
7. Garlic Pickle (1 tsp) {see Chef's in 'METHOD'}
8. Base Gravy (1 Ladle) {1st Ladle}
9. Meat (6~8 pieces) {lamb or chicken or some veggies}
10. Tikka Masala Sauce (1 TBSP) {aka Magic sauce}
11. Salt (½ tsp)
12. Jaggery (1 tsp) {brown sugar will do}
13. Mango Chutney (1 TBSP)
14. Tomato (½) {fresh, chopped}
15. Plum Tomatoes (2) {tinned}
16. Mr Naga Pickle (1 h/tsp)
17. Base Gravy (1 Ladle) {2nd Ladle}
18. Coriander to garnish
19. Butter Ghee (1 TBSP)
20. Tandoori Masala (½ tsp)

METHOD – MR NAGA

1. Heat the pan on a medium flame and add the Oil.
2. Next add the Onions and Methi Leaves and fry together for about a minute.
3. Next add in the Garlic & Ginger Paste and cook off.
4. Now add in the Tomato Paste, 'MIX' Powder and cook on a fairly high heat for about 45 seconds to cook the spices.
5. Next add in the Garlic Pickle.
6. Now, add in the first ladle of Base Gravy.
7. Now, turn down the heat and add in your meat, chicken or vegetables.
8. Next add in the Tikka Masala Sauce and stir in well.
9. Next add Salt, Jaggery and Mango Chutney and stir in.
10. Once the sauce thickens add in the plum and chopped tomatoes, break the plum tomatoes up with your Chef's spoon.
11. Next add in the Mr Naga Pickle.
12. Once the sauce thickens some add in the second ladle of Base gravy.
13. Cook for about another 2-3 minutes then add in the coriander and Ghee and stir in.
14. Turn down the heat and simmer until the Oil rises to the surface.
15. Now add in the Tandoori Masala.

Chef's Note. Garlic Pickle as discussed in the chapter - 'Tips and Trick for restaurant like results' is one of those dish transforming ingredients that when added will make you go, 'Wow!' You can find this in most large Asian grocers or wholesalers, the brands we use in 'Curry 2 Go' are the National brand or Shan. Patak's also do a Garlic Pickle. Use sparingly and always make sure to cook it, in other words don't use this as a finishing spice or ingredient as it will dominate the dish and kill it!

Chicken Tikka Shashlik

 https://youtu.be/S09ultpKX04

This dish is in my opinion basically a Chicken Tikka Masala with personality! If you like Chicken Tikka Masala, you will love this!

Shashlik or Shashlyk {Persian} basically refers to a skewered Kebab. The BIR version is an adaptation of a very popular curry {Chicken Tikka Masala} and tandoor cooked chicken and vegetables. The sauce is often cooked down to a very thick to hardly any sauce type dish. The tandoori cooked meat and vegetables can be cooked under the grill or on a cast iron griddle as demonstrated on my Youtube channel:

INGREDIENTS {in order of use} – CHICKEN TIKKA SHASHLIK

1. Chicken (4~6 large pieces) {pre-marinated in Tikka Masala sauce}
2. Green & Red Peppers (2~4 quarters)
3. Onion (2~4 large chunks)
4. Tomato (1) {halved}
5. Vegetable Oil (1 Chef's spoon)
6. Methi Leaves (1 tsp)
7. Tomato Paste (½ Chef's spoon)
8. Tikka Masala Sauce (2 Chef's spoons) {aka 'Magic' sauce}
9. Base Gravy (½ Ladle) {1st ½ Ladle}
10. Mango Chutney (2 TBSP)
11. Pineapple (6~8 pieces)
12. Pineapple Juice (1 Chef's spoon)
13. Content of Kebab Skewars
14. Base Gravy (½ Ladle) {2nd ½ Ladle}
15. Coconut Flour (1 TBSP)
16. Almond Powder (1 TBSP)
17. Base Gravy (1 Ladle) {2nd Ladle}
18. Single Cream (1 TBSP)
19. Coriander (sprinkle) {Fresh, chopped} [OPTIONAL]

METHOD – CHICKEN TIKKA SHASHLIK

1. Take your marinated Chicken Tikka Pieces, Peppers, Onions and Tomatoes and alternately add onto the skewer.
2. Rub some extra Tikka Masala Sauce onto the meat and vegetable so they are all well coated.
3. Now choose whether to cook this kebab either under the grill or using a griddle pan as shown in the video link in the recipe description.
4. If under the grill, you want to place the kebab on a foil covered tray under a medium to low grill, taking care to keep turning so that the vegetables don't burn and to ensure the meat gets cooked through. {See Chef's notes for a handy tip!}
5. Once the kebab is more or less cooked {not overcooked-very important} set aside.
6. Next take a pan and add the Vegetable Oil, once heated add the Methi Leaves and fry for a few seconds.
7. Next, add the Tomato Paste and the Tikka Masala Sauce and thoroughly mix to combine.
8. Now add half a ladle of Base Gravy and turn up the heat.
9. Next in with the Mango Chutney, Pineapple pieces and juice.
10. Now add kebab ingredients and mix well in the sauce.
11. Next add the other half ladle of base gravy and turn up the heat slightly.
12. Now add in the Coconut Flour and Almond Powder and stir in well.
13. Once the sauce thickens some, add the second ladle of Base Gravy.
14. Turn up the heat and cook the sauce fairly dry, making sure to keep turning the ingredients in the pan.
15. Once the sauce has a thick and glossy quality, serve and garnish with the Single Cream and Coriander [OPTIONAL] ***Done!***

Jeera Tikka Chicken
{Curried Away}

 https://youtu.be/SSaTWoMf3C8

Abdul very kindly shared this recipe with us and for those of you who love the taste of fresh cumin, then you will like this dish. To be honest, it is not my favourite dish but I am sure there are many who will enjoy this.

INGREDIENTS {in order of use} – JEERA TIKKA CHICKEN

1. Vegetable Oil (1 Chef's spoon)
2. Garlic (1~2 cloves) {sliced}
3. Cumin Seed (½ Chef's spoon)
4. Tomato Paste (1 tsp)
5. Onions + Peppers (1 Chef's spoon) {see Adey's magic vegetables}
6. Chicken Tikka (6~8 pieces) {pre-cooked}
7. Tomato Paste (1 Chef's spoon)
8. Methi Leaves (1 tsp)
9. 'MIX' Powder (1 TBSP)
10. Salt (½ tsp)
11. Chilli Powder (½ tsp)
12. Garam Masala (½ tsp)
13. Base Gravy (1 Ladle)
14. Tomato (¼) {fresh, wedge}
15. Coriander (handful) {fresh, chopped}
16. Butter Ghee (½ tsp)

METHOD – JEERA TIKKA CHICKEN

1. First heat the oil in the pan on a medium flame.
2. Add the Garlic and be careful not to brown.
3. Next, add in the Cumin Seeds and toast in the oil for about 45 seconds.
4. Then add about a tsp of Tomato Paste.
5. Put the Onions and Peppers and cook for about a minute.
6. Now add the Chicken pieces and coat in the mixture.
7. Put a Chef's spoon of Tomato Paste then Methi Leaves, 'MIX' Powder, Salt Chilli Powder and Garam Masala.
8. Cook out the spices for about 30 seconds then add the Base Gravy and cook under a high flame.
9. Add in the ¼ wedge of Tomato, fresh Coriander and the Butter Ghee and reduce the heat and serve when the oil rises to the surface. ***Done!***

Southern Indian Garlic Chilli Chicken

About 5 years ago when I lived in Carlisle I used to get a 'tea time special' from a curry house called 'The Flames' on Botchergate. The curry I would always order without fail, was the 'Southern Indian Garlic Chilli Chicken.' It was one of those curries that never failed to satisfy in the taste department as it has everything I like in a curry - namely heat, intense flavour, a nice thick sauce and plenty of it and of course that garlicky taste. In fact, as I write this now I can almost taste that dish! The Pakistani family that owned that takeaway came from Glasgow and it never failed to amuse me when these guys would answer the phone with a broad Glasgow accent and sign off by saying; "Nae bother." I never managed to get the recipe out of them but have adapted my own particular recipe for this dish which I think is close to how they used to make it. This dish requires a 2 part cooking process - the curry and the tarka {spiced oil} added at the end.

INGREDIENTS {in order of use} – SOUTHERN INDIAN GARLIC CHILLI CHICKEN

1. **Seasoned Oil** (1 Chef's spoon)
2. Garlic & Ginger Paste (1 tsp)
3. Methi Leaves (1 tsp)
4. Tomato Paste (1 Chef's spoon)
5. 'MIX' Powder (1 TBSP)
6. Chilli Powder (1 tsp)
7. Salt (½ tsp)
8. Chicken (6~8 pieces) {pre-cooked}
9. Asian Chillies (3~4) {cut in halves length ways}
10. Base Gravy (½ Ladle) {1st half-ladle}
11. Garlic Pickle (1 tsp)
12. Tomato Ketchup (1 TBSP)
13. Mango Chutney (1 TBSP)
14. Base Gravy (½ Ladle) {2nd half-ladle}
15. Tikka Masala Sauce (1 Chef's spoon) {aka Magic Sauce}
16. Base Gravy (1 Ladle) {1st full-ladle}
17. Plum Tomato (1) {tinned + 1 Chef's spoon of juice}
18. Garam Masala (½ tsp)
19. Coriander (handful) {fresh, chopped}
20. Butter Ghee (1 tsp) {for finishing}
21. Tandoori Masala (½ tsp) {after addition of Tarka}

Tarka

1. Butter Ghee (1 TBSP)
2. Vegetable Oil (1 TBSP)
3. Fennel Seeds (½ tsp)
4. Garlic (1 clove) {thinly sliced}

METHOD – SOUTHERN INDIAN GARLIC CHILLI CHICKEN

1. First heat up the pan and oil on a medium flame.
2. Next add in the Garlic & Ginger Paste and fry off.
3. Now add in the Methi Leaves and fry for 30 seconds.
4. Now add in the Tomato Paste and cook out.
5. Next add in the 'MIX' Powder, Chilli Powder and Salt and cook out.
6. Next add in the pre-cooked Chicken and sliced Chillies and mix well.
7. Now add in a half of the first ladle of Base Gravy and turn up the heat slightly.
8. Next add in the Garlic Pickle, Tomato Ketchup and Mango Chutney.
9. Next add in the other half ladle of Base Gravy and stir in.
10. Now add in the Tikka Masala Sauce and stir in well.
11. The sauce should now be thickening so add the second ladle of Base Gravy.
12. Next, add in the Plum Tomato and some of the juice from the can about a Chef's spoon amount.
13. Now add in the Garam Masala and Coriander.
14. Next add the Butter Ghee, mix in, and turn down the heat.

Tarka

Now in a separate pan heat the Butter Ghee and 1 TBSP of Vegetable Oil

Add in the Fennel Seeds, and toast for a few second; next add in the chopped garlic and just as the garlic starts to turn brown and get a bit sticky in the pan empty the contents into the first pan.

Mix in well and sprinkle on the Tandoori Masala. ***Done!***

Chicken Tikka Jafflon {aka Jafflong}

 https://youtu.be/lu_UMtUgxeY

This is a recipe that I have already covered on Youtube thanks to Chef Nural from the Manzil restaurant. This recipe is, per the video link below, apart from the change from pre-cooked Chicken to Chicken Tikka pieces.

INGREDIENTS {in order of use} – CHICKEN TIKKA JAFFLON

1. **Seasoned Oil** (1 Chefs spoon)
2. Garlic & Ginger Paste (1 tsp)
3. Methi Leaves (1 tsp)
4. 'MIX' Powder (1 TBSP)
5. Tomato Paste (1 TBSP)
6. Tandoori Masala (½ tsp)
7. Garam Masala (¼ tsp) {Tad}
8. Salt (¼ tsp) { *not shown in the video!* }
9. Mr Naga Pickle (1 tsp) {scant}
10. Chicken Tikka (6~8 pieces) {pre-cooked}
11. Green Pepper (½) {cut into quarters}
12. **Red Pepper** (½) {cut into quarters}
13. Onion (½) {small, quartered}
14. Base Gravy (1 Ladle)
15. Tomato (1) {small, cut in half}
16. Coriander (sprinkle) {fresh, chopped}
17. Base Gravy (1 Ladle)
18. Coriander to garnish

METHOD – CHICKEN TIKKA JAFFLON

1. Heat the oil in the pan.
2. Now add in the Garlic & Ginger Paste and fry off.
3. Add in the Methi Leaves and 'MIX' Powder.
4. At the same time add in the Tomato Paste, Tandoori Masala, Garam Masala and Salt.
5. Next add in the Mr Naga Pickle.
6. Next add in the Chicken Tikka pieces.
7. Then cook the chicken and those spices, dry for about 30 seconds.
8. Now take the Peppers, Onion and Tomato and deep fry together, at 160°C, for less than a minute just to remove the raw taste, drain and add to the curry.
9. Fry all together then add the first ladle of Base gravy and return to the heat and reduce this sauce until almost dry.
10. Add the fresh coriander to the dish.
11. Once the sauce has reduced to almost nothing add in the final ladle of Base Gravy.
12. Mix in well and cook for another 2-3 minutes.
13. Garnish with fresh coriander and serve. ***Done!***

Saagwala Gosht {or Lamb}

 https://youtu.be/2IOj9LvYY40

This dish is an authentic Indian recipe that has been adapted to the BIR style of curry cooking and is found on the 'Specialities' part of the menu in many a good curry house. I was inspired to make this dish from one of the students I met at the Curry College in Bradford. The traditional dish was made with Mutton - which in India means goat but in Pakistan means sheep, but can be substituted with Lamb; you decide....

This recipe involves a 2-stage cooking process – The Saagwala Sauce and the Curry.

INGREDIENTS {in order of use} – SAAGWALA GOSHT

The Sauce

1. Spinach (100g) {fresh}
2. Coriander (½ bunch) {fresh}
3. Lemon (1) {juice from}
4. Water (¾ Mug)

The Curry

1. **Seasoned Oil** (1 Chef's spoon)
2. Garlic Paste (1 tsp)
3. Methi Leaves (1 tsp)
4. Tomatoes (1 Chefs spoon) {freshly diced}
5. 'MIX' Powder (1 TBSP)
6. Chilli Powder (1 tsp)
7. Base Gravy (1 Ladle)
8. Lamb (6~8 pieces) {pre-cooked, along with some stock}

---

9. Saagwala Sauce (1 Ladle)
10. Salt (½ tsp)
11. Saagwala Sauce (remainder)

METHOD – SAAGWALA GOSHT

The Sauce

1. Add into a blender the spinach, coriander, juice of a Lemon and ¾ of a mug of water.
2. Blitz together until you have a green paste. {You may have to help your blender by stopping the motor and pushing the ingredients down}.
3. Once the Saagwala sauce is a smooth green paste it's done.

The Curry

1. First heat up the oil in a pan and once hot add in the Garlic Paste and Methi Leaves and fry for about 30 seconds.
2. Next add in the fresh Tomatoes, 'MIX' Powder and Chilli Powder.
3. Once the spices are cooked after about 30 seconds add in a ladle of Base Gravy.
4. Next add in the pre-cooked lamb and mix in well.
5. Now turn up the heat and cook until the sauce thickens.
6. Add about a Ladle of Saagwala Sauce and turn up the heat to high and cook the sauce into the curry.
7. The curry should start to turn a green colour, after 2 minutes of cooking add the Salt and the remainder of the Saagwala Sauce and reduce the heat to a simmer.
8. Serve and garnish with fresh chopped Coriander. ***Done!***

Adey's 4-min Chicken Korma

 https://youtu.be/LgMexBISDdM

INGREDIENTS & METHOD {in order of use} – CHICKEN KORMA

1. Base Gravy (1½ Ladles) {In a pan on a medium=>high heat}
2. Korma Sauce (1 H/Chef's spoon)
3. Chicken (8 pieces) {pre-cooked}
4. Single Cream (3~4 TBSP) {cook until the pre-cooked chicken has been completely heated through}
5. Butter Ghee (1 tsp) {added at end for gloss} [OPTIONAL]

Adey's Korma Sauce

 https://youtu.be/ctdQfB4KKL4

INGREDIENTS & METHOD {in order of use} – KORMA SAUCE

1. Onions (¼ filled) {finely sliced in a 5 Litre Pan}
2. Raisen & Sultana Mix (2 Chef's spoons)
3. Garlic & Ginger Paste (½ Chef's spoon)
4. Vegetable Oil (½ Chef's spoon)
5. Butter Ghee (½ Chef's spoon)
6. Heat-up and ensure Onions are fully coated with the mix.
7. Water (as reqd) {Cover the onions and simmer covered until the Onions have completely disintegrated!}
8. Blend cooled mixture until very very smooth.
9. Now add (equal quantities) {by volume} of Castor Sugar, Almond Powder, Coconut Flour and Single Cream. {The actual quantities required are determined by the consistency of the mix – PlayDough?}

Chef's Note. The Korma Sauce can be frozen into 'single-portions' for future use.

Chicken Tikka Moghul

 https://youtu.be/igerXmf9MvY

INGREDIENTS {in order of use} – CHICKEN TIKKA MOGHUL

1. Butter Ghee (½ Chef's spoon)
2. Vegetable Oil (½ Chef's spoon)
3. Garlic Cloves (3) {finely sliced}
4. Onion (¼) {sliced}
5. **Red Pepper** (1 slice)
6. Green Pepper (3 slices)
7. Methi Leaves (sprinkle)
8. Garlic Paste (1 tsp)
9. Tomato Paste (1 Chef's spoon)
10. 'MIX' Powder (1 TBSP)
11. Salt (1 pinch)
12. Chilli Powder (½ tsp)
13. Garam Masala (½ tsp)
14. Cumin Seeds (½ tsp)
15. Base Gravy (½ Ladle)
16. Chicken Tikka (8 pieces) {pre-cooked sliced breast}
17. Coriander (sprinkle) {fresh}
18. Adey's Tikka Masala Sauce (1 H/Chef's spoon) {or Tikka Masala Sauce from Part 1}
19. Adey's Korma Sauce (½ Chef's spoon)
20. Base Gravy (1 Ladle)
21. Single Cream (3~4 Chef's spoons) {ignore Julian's "tablespoons"}
22. Mr Naga Pickle (½ tsp)
23. Sugar (1 TBSP) {white granulated}
24. Lime (¼) {squeeze juice from then add to pan}
25. Coriander (sprinkle) {fresh}
26. Butter Ghee (½ TBSP) {for glossy finish}
27. Garam Masala (sprinkle)
28. Serve and garnish with a 'line of single cream' and flaked almonds

---

METHOD – CHICKEN TIKKA MOGHUL

1. Add the Butter Ghee and Oil to a heated pan on a medium flame.
2. Add the Garlic, Onions and Peppers followed by a pinch of Methi Leaves.
3. Add the Garlic Paste and cook out.
4. Then add the Tomato Paste and cook out.
5. Now add the spices: 'MIX' Powder, Salt, Chilli Powder, Garam Masala and Cumin Seeds and then cook out the spices.
6. Then add half-ladle of Base Gravy and mix in.
7. Now add the Chicken Tikka pieces and gentle coat with the mix.
8. Add the Coriander and Tikka Masala Sauce, Korma Sauce and a ladle of Base Gravy and thoroughly combine the pan's contents.
9. Add the Single Cream and combine.
10. Add the Mr Naga Pickle.
11. Add the sugar and mix in.
12. Squeeze the juice from a wedge of Lime and add the Lime to the pan.
13. Finish the dish off with some fresh Coriander, Butter Ghee and a pinch of Garam Masala.
14. Serve up and garnish with a dribble of Single Cream and some Flaked Almonds. ***Done!***

Garlic Prawns on Puri

 https://youtu.be/7ktwCjWL6RI

INGREDIENTS {in order of use} – GARLIC PRAWNS ON PURI

1. Butter Ghee (1 Chef's spoon) {scant}
2. **Seasoned Oil** (1 tsp)
3. Garlic (3 cloves) {finely sliced}
4. Onion + Pepper Mix (good handful) {sliced}
5. Tomato Paste (1 Chef's spoon) {scant}
6. Tomato + Cucumber Mix (handful)
7. Prawns (2 Chef's spoons) {pre-cooked}
8. Spring Onion (1 TBSP) {chopped}
9. Coriander (good sprinkle) {fresh, chopped}
10. Methi Leaves (pinch)
11. 'MIX' Powder (1 TBSP) {scant}
12. Salt (½ tsp)
13. Chilli Powder (½ tsp)
14. Garam Masala (pinch)
15. Base Gravy (½ Ladle)
16. Tomato Paste (½ Chef's spoon) {for colour}
17. Mr Naga Pickle (½ tsp)[OPTIONAL]
18. Base Gravy (½ Ladle)
19. Chaat Masala (2 sprinkles)
20. Coriander (sprinkle) {fresh, chopped}
21. Tomato (¼) {fresh, wedge}
22. Butter Ghee (1 tsp)

METHOD – GARLIC PRAWNS ON PURI

1. Heat the Butter Ghee and Seasoned Oil in a pan and add the sliced Garlic and cook just before browning.
2. Add the onion and Pepper Mix and cook some before adding the Tomato Paste.
3. Add the Tomato and Cucumber Mix and cook out before adding the pre-cooked prawns.
4. Add the Spring Onion, Coriander, Methi Leaves, 'MIX' Powder, Salt, Chilli Powder and Garam Masala and cook out the spices whilst coating the prawns.
5. Add the first half-ladle of Base Gravy and mix the contents throughly.
6. Add the Tomato Paste {for colour} and the Mr Naga Pickle before adding the 2nd half-ladle of Base Gravy.
7. Finally add the Chaat Masala, Coriander, Tomato Wedge and finish with a dribble of Butter Ghee.
8. The Puri is made from Chapatti Dough that is rolled out and deep fried, in seasoned oil, at 160°C for around 20 seconds, being turned during cooking. Place on some kitchen towel to absorb the excess oil.
9. The dish is finished by topping the Puri with the Prawn Curry and finished off with coriander, cucumber, dribble of single cream and a sprinkle of Chaat Masala.

Chef's Note. The recipe for making the Chapati dough is in our sister publication: *'The secret to that Takeaway Curry Taste PART 1'*

Staff Fish Curry {Curried Away}

 https://youtu.be/iK7KNA50fQk

After a busy day of filming, Adey kindly made us this curry and I have to say it was delicious. It also got Abdul's approval which says something as Bengalis eat more fish than meat, so it had to be good to get his thumbs up. Here is the recipe:

INGREDIENTS {in order of use} – STAFF FISH CURRY

1. Tilapia (3~4 fillets) {Fresh or frozen {defrosted} - pre-marinated in a little Turmeric powder, Garlic & Ginger Paste and fresh Coriander}
2. **Seasoned Oil** (½ a Chef's spoon)
3. Butter Ghee (½ a Chef's spoon)
4. Chilli (1 large) {Red - dried}
5. Bay Leaves (3)
6. Cinnamon (1~2 sticks)
7. Cardamom (3~4) {Green}
8. Chillies (3~4) {Green - sliced}
9. Star Anise (1~2 petals) {Crushed}
10. Cumin Seed (½ tsp) {Black}
11. Cloves (2)
12. Cardamom (1) {Black – crushed}
13. Garlic (2 cloves) {Fresh – sliced}
14. Scotch Bonnet Chilli Pepper (1) {Diced}
15. Red Chilli Flakes (1 Pinch)
16. Cumin Seeds (1 Pinch) {Brown}
17. Tomato Paste (1 Chef's spoon)
18. Saffron (a few strands) {Soaked in a little water} [OPTIONAL]
19. Methi Leaves (1 Pinch)
20. Salt (½ tsp)
21. 'MIX' Powder (1 TBSP)
22. Coriander (handful) {Fresh}
23. Chopped Onions (2 Chef's spoons)
24. Lemon Juice (good squeeze) {Fresh}

---

25. Water (1 glass)
26. Marinated Fish
27. Garam Masala (Sprinkle)
28. Tomato (3~4 quarters)
29. Coriander {Fresh - to garnish}
30. Butter Ghee (1 TBSP) {Added at the end}
31. Lemon (2~3 slices) {Fresh} [OPTIONAL]

METHOD – STAFF FISH CURRY

1. Heat the Vegetable Oil and Ghee in the pan on a medium heat.
2. Next add in the whole spices {except the brown cumin seeds}
3. Also add in the fresh garlic and the scotch bonnet chilli pepper.
4. Fry everything together moving the ingredients around the pan so as to avoid burning the spices.
5. Next add in the brown cumin seeds.
6. Now add in the Tomato Paste and cook out.
7. Next add the Saffron and a pinch of Methi.
8. Next add in the Salt and the 'MIX' Powder and stir in.
9. Add in a little water to keep things from drying out.
10. Now add in the fresh coriander.
11. Next add in about 2 Chef's spoons of chopped onions.
12. Now add in a good squeeze of fresh lemon juice.
13. Next add in one glass of water to help soften the onions.
14. Once the onions have cooked a little more add in the fish.
15. Next add in the Garam Masala and tomato quarters and cook for another 3 minutes to reduce the sauce.
16. Serve with plain rice or chapattis. ***Done!***

Chicken Bhuna {Curried Away}

 https://youtu.be/3GFThKZSOoY

INGREDIENTS {in order of use} – CHICKEN BHUNA

1. **Seasoned Oil** (1 Chef's spoon)
2. Garlic & Ginger Paste (1 tsp) { *not in video commentary*}
3. Tomato Paste (1 Chef's spoon)
4. Methi Leaves (½ tsp)
5. 'MIX' Powder (1 TBSP)
6. Salt (pinch)
7. Garam Masala (pinch)
8. Chilli Powder (½ tsp) {or adjust to taste}
9. Base Gravy (½ ladle) { *not in video commentary*}
10. Onions + Peppers (good handful) {diced - see Adey's 'Magic' vegetables}
11. Chicken (6~8 pieces) {pre-cooked with some of the stock}
12. Tomato (½) {2 quarter wedges}
13. Coriander (good sprinkle) {fresh, chopped}
14. Base Gravy (1 Ladle)
15. Mr Naga Pickle (½ tsp)
16. Coriander (good sprinkle) {fresh, chopped - 2nd helping}
17. Butter Ghee (1 tsp)
18. Garam Masala (sprinkle) {finishing spice}
19. Garnish with fresh Coriander and a ¼ wedge of fresh Tomato.

METHOD – CHICKEN BHUNA

1. Add oil to the hot pan.
2. Add the Garlic & Ginger Paste and cook out for 30 seconds.
3. Next add in the Tomato Paste and cook out.
4. Now in with the spices: Methi Leaves, 'MIX' Powder, Salt, Garam Masala & Chilli Powder.
5. Add ½ Ladle of Base Gravy to loosen the mix.
6. Now mix together and cook the spices over a high heat.
7. Next in with the Onion and Peppers and fry together.
8. Now in with the pre-cooked Chicken and some stock.
9. Add in to 2 Tomato quarters and fresh Coriander.
10. Next add in a ladle of Base Gravy and cook the mixture for 2 minutes.
11. Next add in the Mr Naga Pickle.
12. Add another sprinkle of fresh Coriander.
13. Add some Butter Ghee.
14. When the oil floats to the surface serve-up and garnish with fresh Coriander and a quarter wedge of fresh Tomato. ***Done!***

Chapter 7

More Insights, Tips and Recipes

As I was coming to the end of writing Part 2 *to 'The Secret to That Takeaway Curry Taste'* I realised that there were things I wanted to mention but that perhaps didn't fit into any of the other chapters I had wrote thus far, plus I forgot one or two things; hence this chapter - more Insights, Tips and Recipes.

There is one secret ingredient that I couldn't add to this book and that ingredient is **you.**

Yes, you are perhaps the missing ingredient to achieving the true BIR taste that you are searching for, in other words you need to not only take these recipes and techniques and cook them - you need to *practice, practice, and practice.* I hope I have helped you come to appreciate that this vital missing ingredient is ultimately what is going to get you there. I sincerely hope that the two books I have written with the title - *'The Secret to That Takeaway Curry Taste'* help *you* achieve that *taste.* I hope that my experience along with Adey's, helps you create dishes that will impress the toughest critic. I won't be writing any more BIR style cookbooks - so there will be no Part 3 as I think I have covered pretty much everything I know and have learned from my own twenty years experience in searching for and achieving that British Indian Restaurant taste.

So here are a few final thoughts and ideas to top it all.

Finishing Dishes

As you will have noted many dishes have something added at the end to 'Finish the dish, for example Garam Masala, Ghee, Coriander, some other spice or spiced oil. Some Chef's make this spiced oil and add a drizzle of this at the end of the cooking process to impart that extra something. I wouldn't recommend 'Seasoned Oil' for this purpose but why not try Adey's seasoned oil shortcut' or try making a flavoured oil of your own. One I have seen is Garlic Oil. It's easy to make, you just take some vegetable oil say about 250 ml, then take some Garlic paste {homemade is better - see Adey's video below} then add to the Oil 1 TBSP of Garlic Paste and whisk together well. Leave the oil for about 2 days then pour it through some cheese cloth so as to filter out the bits and you will have amazing tasting oil! You can add this to dishes like Garlic Chicken or any spicy curry just at the end, say about ½ tsp.

Ghee also has the ability to enrich a dish and many Chefs add Ghee to dishes like Moghul, Korma, Butter Chicken and so forth; Ghee adds a rich nutty flavour and a gloss to the finished dish.

Kashmiri Masala Oil is another one. We use it at 'Curry 2 Go' and I mentioned in my first e-book with regard to the Pillau rice recipe, however this very aromatic tasting oil can be used in curries and other cooked dishes, so why not experiment.

Garam Masala Oil. This oil is made by adding Garam spices - usually, Cinnamon, Cloves, Cardamom {black & green}, whole Coriander Seeds, Fennel Seeds, brown Cumin Seeds, Nutmeg, Black Pepper Corns and dried Red Kashmiri (or type) Chillies.

The way to make this aromatic oil, say a small amount about 200ml is to take 1 H/TBSP of Coriander, 1 TBSP of Cumin Seeds, 4 Cloves, 6 Green Cardamom and 2 black, 2 x 75mm pieces of stick Cinnamon or Acacia Bark, 6 Black Pepper Corns, 1 tsp of Fennel Seeds and 2-3 Kashmiri Chillies. Heat the whole spices very gently over a low flame to release the volatile oils for about 5-8 minutes making sure to keep them moving in the pan so as not to burn them, then while the spices are still warm add them to the 200ml of oil in a jug and give it a good stir. Next pour the oil into a caped bottle and give it a good shake. The longer you leave the oil the better, you will need to leave this for at least 3 days before use. The way to use this is to add it as a finishing ingredient say a curry just as before it's about to be served - say a tsp per portion. The great thing about flavoured oils is the subtle taste level they add to the dish which is different from the powdered spice. I have noticed some of the more 'a la carte' style 'Indian' restaurant use flavoured oils as opposed to just powdered spices to finish a dish.

Scorching

Have you ever ordered a speciality dish that comes on a sizzler? You might think it's just a gimmick or a bit of theatre, which it is, yet the effect of taking a pan cooked dish and adding it into a scorching hot cast iron sizzler is that of adding a charred taste to the dish. You can try this technique at home using a cast iron Karahi which you should be able to find at a good Asian store {they sell everything!} just put it in a hot oven for ten minutes then {with some good oven gloves} carefully take out the dish and place it on a wooden chopping board and then pour in your curry. This will have the effect of scorching the outer layer of the curry and adding that charred or smoky taste.

Coconut Cream

Some Bengali Chefs add coconut cream {in a block} into the Base gravy to add a layer of flavour. I have tried this Base recipe at 'Curry 2 Go' and I think it's OK and works well with certain dishes but not others. Why not add a TBSP of coconut milk {canned variety} to you Masala dishes or Korma, it can also work really well in a Madras. In fact the first Madras recipe I ever learned to cook had the inclusion of coconut milk in it and it worked really well.

Panch Puren

As with the case of Adey's Bombay Aloo recipe, Panch Puren {5 Spice} can be added to vegetable dishes to add that edge or bitterness, just make sure the spices are cooked or they will overpower the dish and just add a sprinkle; don't get carried away!

Green Chillies

In more authentic style Indian cooking green chillies are used more for flavour than heat, they add a heady pungent type heat to a dish and often they add these generously to many a dish. If you remove the seeds and chop them very fine {slit in half, length ways then scrape out the seeds then chop across the chilli vertically} they become almost like a spice to the dish. Asian households buy these by the kilo so they need to keep well. A tip is to remove the stem and keep them in a paper bag in a cupboard not in the fridge and they will last for well over a week.

Onions

If you will be peeling a lot of onions and they always make you cry, simply soak the peeled un-chopped onions in cold water for 10 minutes first and you won't have any problems.

Garlic & Ginger Paste

 https://youtu.be/6zOb9ebJi3g

To make this paste last longer, a restaurant trick is to add some hot oil {50ml} to the freshly blended mixture {500g} and a tsp of Salt and this keeps it fresher longer; it also stops it going green.

Perfect Rice

Here is a restaurant trick for perfect rice with nice separate grains: add a TBSP of Lemon Juice and a TBSP of Oil to the boiling water and this will give you perfect separate grains.

Adey's Perfect Pillau Rice

 https://youtu.be/iyHgM3pPGqc

Staff Curries

Many of you will be familiar with 'Staff Curries' in other words the curries the staff eat as they generally don't eat anything off the menu as BIR style curry is not to their taste. BIR restaurants and takeaways are now putting these on the menu because people are asking for them. This excerpt was taken from a Takeaway called 'Cinnamon'

LOOKING FOR SOMETHING DIFFERENT?

At Cinnamon we are always trying to bring fresh innovative dishes to our customers. Our chef's have created these authentic Bangladeshi Staff curries, which are truly authentic curries as you will get. So called staff curries because they are based on traditional home cooked curries for staff to eat at the end of the night, hence the unusual name. These dishes will truly enhance your experience of Indian food dining with their authentic flavours, textures & the taste of whole & ground spices as you've never had before.

As I have been getting quite a few requests for these type of recipes, I have included a Staff Fish Curry in Chapter 6 and a rice dish called Kitcheree follows.

Kitcheree

This simple but incredibly tasty rice and bean dish can be eaten as a complete meal by itself as you have a perfect balance of carbohydrates, proteins and fat - mixed with some spices to make it taste great. I love this dish and make it in my house almost every week and it gets a big thumbs up from the rest of the family.

 https://youtu.be/rXz0qn7z8Vw

INGREDIENTS {in order of use} - KITCHEREE {serves 3~4}

1. Mung Beans (1 mug) {Pre-soaked for at least 4 hours}
2. Water (2 mugs)
3. Ghee (1½ Chef's spoons)
4. Cumin Seed (1 h/tsp)
5. Curry Leaves (a few)
6. Green Chillies (3~4) {chopped}
7. Onions (2) {Small, chopped}
8. Garlic & Ginger Paste (1 TBSP)
9. Basmati Rice (1 mug) {Washed and drained}
10. Mung Beans (1 mug) {cooked at paras 1 and 2 above}
11. Water (½ mug)
12. Stock {from the mung beans}
13. Salt (1 tsp)

METHOD - KITCHEREE

1. First, take the soaked Mung Beans and put them in a pressure cooker with 2 mugs of Water and bring to pressure, then cook at pressure for 1 minute. Take off the heat and allow the pressure to dissipate naturally and once cooled, empty the contents of the pressure cooker and *set aside for use later.*
2. In an *empty* pressure cooker, add the Butter Ghee and once hot add in the Cumin Seeds, Curry Leaves and the Green Chillies.
3. Now add the Onions and cook these till they turn translucent.
4. Then add the Garlic & Ginger Paste and cook until the Onions start to turn brown.
5. Next add in the Rice and fry in the mixture till the rice grains all turn white.
6. Now add in the Mung Beans and stir in, fry for 1 minute.
7. Now add the Water, Mung Bean Stock and the Salt.
8. Next, stir the mixture once and on with the pressure cooker lid.
9. Bring to pressure then *straight off the heat.*
10. Leave the mixture to steam in the residual pressure for 10 minutes.
11. After 10 minutes, release the lid and fluff up the rice with a fork.

Engladeshi Food

"What is that?" I here you say. Well actually most things on the BIR menu.

Actually, I first heard the term 'Engladeshi' from Adey at Curried Away. He used the term to describe food that was a fusion of both English and Bangladeshi food - hence 'Engladeshi.' One such recipe which I just had to add in this book is Adey's Marmite & Cheese Naan bread. Now before you laugh, seriously this is a great combination! You have a perfect marriage of delicious soft white hot Naan bread, spread thinly with marmite (you either love it or hate it!) top with cheddar cheese. I must admit when Adey raved on about it saying I had to try it I was sceptical, however he made us this at the end of a busy day's filming and I have to honestly say it was delicious! Obviously this was made in a tandoor oven, but you could make the Naan the way I show you on my Youtube channel, see here:

 https://youtu.be/ro_LGuzwMc0

After making the Naan, spread on the Marmite, then sprinkle with Cheddar Cheese, place under the grill just till the cheese melts. Yummy!

Adey's Marmite & Cheese Naan bread

 https://youtu.be/gPcthj99yAA

More 'Engladeshi' Food...

When making tomato based curries like Rogan Josh, Madras or South Indian Chilli Chicken, if the tomatoes are not very ripe or good quality (say in winter) add in 2 TBSP of tomato ketchup - this is a trick a Bengali Chef showed me and it works a treat - true 'Engladeshi' taste!

When making Chicken Tikka Masala try adding in half a small can of Heinz Cream of Tomato Soup and a little less Base Gravy - you won't believe how good it tastes!

Baked beans are used to make a dip you sometimes get in the pickle tray to have with your Poppadoms. Here is how you make it:

INGREDIENTS & METHOD - DIP

1. Baked Beans (½ tin) {with sauce}
2. Plum Tomatoes (½ tin)
3. Lemon Dressing (2 TBSP)
4. Methi Leaves (1 h/tsp)
5. Mango Chutney (2 TBSP)
6. Chilli Powder (1 Pinch)
7. Chaat Masala (1 Pinch)

Simply blend all the ingredients together well, add a little water for a more sauce like consistency - this is a really nice dip.

Birds Custard Powder

This is sometimes used in Bhajis, Pakoras or any gram flour type starter. It is used to add sweet creamy taste to the batter - *and it really does!* If making a batch of say 10 onion Bhajis just add in a TBSP for noticeably great results.

ALL GOOD THINGS COME TO AN END...

I couldn't finish this book without a word about 'Curry 2 Go' in Chorley and passing on the torch to Ratchada. In March 2011 Katy, my wife, had to stay in the hospital with our youngest son Zac after he developed Cellulites and was in the hospital for a week. At the time my wife was full of a cold. After leaving the hospital with Zac, Katy's health deteriorated and the Doctor told us she "just had a bad virus..." within two days she was in the hospital on a life support machine with double pneumonia and septicaemia. She was in a coma for almost a month and we were told to expect the worst. What had happened was that she had become run down, I believe from the hectic life we were living at the time running 'Curry 2 Go' and caring for three children, one of which is disabled. We later learned that when she had stayed in the hospital with Zac she had contracted a 'superbug' which was resistant to antibiotics - hence she nearly died from Pneumonia - *aren't hospitals supposed to make you well?*

Thankfully with the excellent care of the Doctors and Nurses in the Hospital as well as a lot of prayers, Katy made a full recovery. I couldn't help but feel guilty at that time about the fact that I had taken on this Takeaway business - which yes, fulfilled a dream of mine but now required my wife to work almost full time in supporting me running this business. Add to that looking after three kids and a home.

While she was in the hospital for the first two weeks I simply shut the takeaway, however after two weeks needs must be met and I opened it again. My 19 year old daughter Hannah quit her job and helped her Dad out. I remember feeling that I didn't want to step foot in that place partly because it had lost its appeal but also because I suppose I blamed the place for what had just happened to Katy.

We both had put so much into that business and worked such long hours to make it pay. I had quit my previous business as a Satellite TV Engineer and put everything we had into this venture and now I couldn't stomach the thought of stepping foot inside there.

What should I do? I prayed about it and made my decision. I told some local neighbouring businesses of my intent to sell up and within just seven days I had a phone call from the Market Manager saying he had the number of an interested person to call. I called a lady named Ratchada, a Thai lady who was looking for a business to develop. We met at 'Curry 2 Go', she looked at my books then asked me what I wanted for the Business, I told her and she gave me a cash deposit there and then. It was sold. She offered me an extra amount of money to stay on for four more weeks to train her in BIR curry as she wanted to keep most of my menu as well as add to it with her own Thai curries - hence the name 'Curry 2 Go' would stay. I suppose that thought pleased me at the time.

After four weeks I left 'Curry 2 Go' in her hands and as I walked through Chorley Town centre that afternoon I had a heavy heart because I knew my curry cooking career was effectively over. I was also unemployed and wasn't sure what to do with myself. I spent the first few weeks of my new found unemployment looking after Katy, decorating the house and finishing a new bathroom we had had fitted as a surprise for Katy.

I kept my eye on 'Curry 2 Go' over the next few weeks helping Ratchada along the way, I would pop in now and then and do a quick shift to help her through a busy spell - all for the price of a few free curries!

Over the next two months the focus of our family changed, we came to appreciate the fact that you can't take health and therefore your life for granted. We had had a close call and we felt as if we had been given a second chance.

I began looking more into the causes of health and also the causes of illness and as a result of that we made some pretty radical changes in the Voigt household and subsequently all our health improved. The fact that my e-book - *'The Secret to That Takeaway Curry Taste'* was selling quite well gave us a breather allowing me to figure out what to do about work.

Eventually I decided that It was best to go back to what I knew and my trade as an Aerial & Satellite TV Engineer. This trade had served me well for years and provided our family with a comfortable income; it also meant that I could support the family financially while my wife could stay at home looking after the kids and everything else. I have now been back doing this job for over 12 months and everything is working out just fine.

Why then did I write, *'The Secret to That Takeaway Curry Taste Part 2'?* Well, I had already mentioned in Part 1 that I had planned to write a second book with many more BIR style recipes as well as some more tips and insights and before Katy got sick, while I was still running 'Curry 2 Go', I had made a start on Part 2 but now here I was months later our life having been turned upside down and without my Curry business.

One Sunday afternoon I was layed on the bed having a bit of a 'wet pillow' and I suddenly remembered Adey. Adey had been in contact with me regularly after buying my e-book, telling me of his passion for Curry and his desire to sell his Burger vans and open an 'Indian' Takeaway. I had encouraged him to go for it. Having bought his takeaway and employed two Bengali chefs he was from time to time e-mailing me with insights he was gaining into BIR cooking; he kept inviting me over to Boston in Lincolnshire to get together. Well this Sunday afternoon after my snooze it suddenly came to me; *"Why not finish the second book and include Adey in the project!"* I rang him there and then and he was more than enthusiastic. I was happy because I had felt as if there was still some 'unfinished business.'

Well, business is finished. I hope you have enjoyed my books - The Secret to That Takeaway Curry Taste Part 1 & 2 and I hope that these books have given you more insight into the wonderful world of British Indian Restaurant cuisine.

I hope these books have inspired you, perhaps who knows to open your own curry business like I did and like Adey and many others have done who bought my first e-book.

Will there be any more Curry books? No - well certainly none about BIR curry anyway. As I have already mentioned in this chapter I feel I have shared with you everything I know. Thankfully there are others now writing their own e-books and making Youtube videos sharing what they have discovered, so I am sure more insight and recipes will be revealed.

I want to thank Adey and Curried Away for their involvement in this book and for his support. I want to thank everyone who has taken the time to let me know what they think of my e-book and Youtube videos. Will I keep making videos for my channel? Yes, but perhaps one every month or so as I find the time. You may though see some more of me on Youtube in the near future...

As I mentioned in a blog on my website quite a few months back about a plan to launch a new Youtube channel about Health and Healthy Recipes. I have been working on this concept with a close friend of mine for the past 8 months and there will be news of that soon on my Curry Youtube channel.

FINAL THOUGHTS...

People often ask me, "how did you learn so much about BIR cooking?" The answer, I asked people! Yes, I made it my aim to find out what I wanted to know and every time I was in an 'Indian' restaurant or takeaway I would ask them for some recipes or tips or I might ask If I could meet the Chef and see my dish being made. Obviously I had a few polite refusals but if you ask enough you will undoubtedly get some answers. Youtube is now becoming an authority on almost anything and more Indian restaurant owners and Chefs are posting videos and recipes.

When it comes to your own cooking I am going to re-iterate what I have already said many times over and that is, practice, practice and practice some more!

As somebody once wisely put it, "If at first you don't succeed try, try and try again."

Happy currying!

26263758R00080

Printed in Great Britain
by Amazon